THE
VICTORIAN
VILLAGE

THE
VICTORIAN
VILLAGE

David Souden

Brockhampton Press

For my parents

Half-title illustration: *A thatched cottage in the village of Marston Sicca in Gloucestershire.*
Frontispiece: *May Day by Thomas Chambers. The village children go off to the May Day celebrations*
with their posies and garlands. A May Day song from Cornwall goes, 'Unite, unite, let us all unite /
For Summer is a-come unto day / And whither we are going we will all unite /
On the merry morning of May.'

This edition published 1995 by Brockhampton Press,
a member of Hodder Headline PLC Group

ISBN 1 86019 141 X

First published in Great Britain in 1991
by Collins & Brown Limited

Copyright © Collins & Brown 1991

Text copyright © David Souden,
Elizabeth Drury and Philippa Lewis 1991

Conceived, edited and designed by Collins & Brown

Editorial Director: **Gabrielle Townsend**
Managing Editor: **Elizabeth Drury**
Editor: **Jennifer Chilvers**
Picture Research: **Philippa Lewis**
Art Director: **Roger Bristow**
Designer: **Ruth Hope**

Filmset by August Filmsetting
Reproduction by Scantrans, Singapore
Printed and bound in Great Britain by BPC Hazells Books Ltd

CONTENTS

INTRODUCTION

GEORGE ELIOT WROTE ONE of the classic descriptions of an English village: '...with a neat or handsome parsonage and grey church set in the midst; there was the pleasant tinkle of the blacksmith's anvil, the patient carthorses waiting at his door; the basket-maker peeling his willow wands in the sunshine; the wheelwright putting the last touch to a blue cart with red wheels; here and there a cottage with bright transparent windows showing pots full of blooming balsams or geraniums, and little gardens in front all double daisies or dark wallflowers; at the well, clean comely women carrying yoked buckets, and towards the free school small Britons dawdling on, and handling their marbles in the pockets of unpatched corduroys adorned with brass buttons.'

Villagers take shelter in a barn with the animals in the painting by Robert Hills, 'A Village in Snow'. Down the main street, past an inn, a herd of cattle is being driven as the snowflakes fall.

Victorian writers and artists described the village and the countryside in many ways and moods: sometimes sentimental, sometimes outraged; sometimes concerned, sometimes condescending; occasionally amused and always intrigued. With contemporary pictures that reflect some of the writers' feelings, and enhance their observations, we celebrate the Victorian village.

The most thorough transformation of England, relative to the length of the period, probably took place during Queen Victoria's reign. When the queen came to the throne in 1837, the nation was primarily rural: two-thirds of the population lived in the countryside. By 1851, half of the English population lived in towns, and by 1901 the figure was more than three-quarters.

Most rural areas, where the population had been growing rapidly for sixty years or more, saw numbers begin to fall after the 1850s and 1860s. Many villages on the eve of the First World War were smaller than they had been at the beginning of the Napoleonic Wars, and they were certainly smaller than when Victoria became queen.

As the towns grew, a nostalgia for rural life developed: most townspeople, after all, had their roots in the country and had memories of visits to grandparents on the farm or in the village. Artists set up easels to paint picturesque views of cottages and their gardens, and of cottagers themselves, feeding ducks by the

pond, fetching water, tending their vegetables, picking flowers. With town-dwelling purchasers in mind, they would subtly alter what they saw to conform to prevailing notions of what the country was like.

Writers, too, captured the old rural ways at a time when they were fast disappearing. There were some who regarded country life harshly, noticing and condemning the poverty that existed, and others who saw it in a golden light. 'How delightful it is in these sweet summer evenings to wander from cottage to cottage and from farm to farm exchanging bright words and looks with the beautiful girls at their garden gates and talking to the kindly people sitting at their cottage doors or meeting in the lane when their work is done,' wrote Francis Kilvert in his diary in 1875. 'How sweet it is to pass from house to house welcome and beloved everywhere by young and old.' Artists and writers provide us with a picture of village life both as it was and as they wished it to be in Victorian times.

THE VILLAGE

The Cotswold village of Broadway, painted at the end of the nineteenth century by William Harris. By this period the wool trade, on which the prosperity of the area was founded, was waning; but the village still appears to be thriving, with several shops visible along the main street. The width of the street reflects the fact that Broadway was on the main droving route from Wales, and herds of cattle and sheep would have been driven down it on their way to the London market.

'A SMALL NEIGHBOURHOOD is as good in sober waking reality as in poetry or prose; a village neighbourhood, such as this Berkshire hamlet in which I write, a long, straggling, winding street at the bottom of a fine eminence, with a road through it, always abounding in carts, horsemen, and carriages, and lately enlivened by a stagecoach from B. to S., which passed through some ten days ago, and will I suppose return some time or other... Will you walk with me through our village, courteous reader? The journey is not long.'

Thus Mary Russell Mitford opened the first of her gentle essays about *Our Village*, describing Three Mile Cross, near Reading in Berkshire, shortly before Queen Victoria's accession in 1837. As she went through her village, she passed tiny cottages where labouring families lived, the shoemaker's and the blacksmith's houses, the village shop, 'multifarious as a bazaar', the inn, the dwellings of a few better-off retired people, the village carpenter's, the home of the gardener at a large house nearby. In Miss Mitford's village, the main lane snaked its way through, reaching the common with more cottages ranged around it.

Not every village was like hers. By 1901, when Queen Victoria died, there were in any case fewer craftsmen in a typical English village because of the effects of the Industrial Revolution. Furthermore, most villages did not have a good road running through. The important roads had a macadamized surface of small, compacted stones, and usually a turnpike road governed by a trust. Other country roads were frequently of stones and gravel, while lanes and tracks had dirt surfaces, white with dust in summer and deep with mud in winter. Stone-breaking and road-mending were among the menial chores that elderly or unemployed men, or indeed convicts, had to do in Victorian England. Deeply-rutted surfaces made road travel uncomfortable, and

country people who could afford a horse-drawn vehicle would buy a cart with springs. As they passed along the country lanes, they might encounter children at play, dogs that ran alongside, hens pecking in the dust, and animals being driven from field to field or to market.

A great change in the organization of land and farms had taken place in many parts of the country in the fifty years before Queen Victoria came to the throne. A great swathe of countryside through southern and midland England had been enclosed: open fields, communally owned and farmed in strips, and common lands, were divided up and made into individual fields for separate farms. The ancient network of tracks that had led into and around the large fields disappeared, and new roads were planned by the enclosure commissioners. They may still be seen crossing the countryside, with hawthorn hedges and wide verges on either side, straight (drawn on the map with a ruler), and altering course only when they meet the roads of the next parish at the boundary. It was as a result of the enclosure movement that farmers in some parts of the country moved out of their farmhouses in the centre of the village and on to their newly reorganized landholdings.

The appearance of the villages reflected the character of the land, for they were built with the materials that were to be obtained locally: in stone where there were quarries nearby, in brick where there was clay suitable for brickmaking, or in timber or even wattle and daub. Similarly, roofs were made of stone, slate, tiles or thatch. 'There is something indescribably cosy about a thatched roof,' wrote Stewart Dick. 'It seems to wrap a house

Villages varied considerably in their layout and appearance. Some, like Sevenhampton, Gloucestershire (below left), consisted of cottages clustering around a green, whereas in the village of Ewelme, in Oxfordshire (below), farmhouses, cottages and the almshouses stretch out along the hillside below the big house.

round like a blanket, and speaks convincingly of warmth and comfort. It softens out all the angularities from the roof-lines, smooths them over with the gentle curves of a snow-drift; the dormer windows become little peep-holes like birds' nests, and the overhanging eaves are full of sparrows.' The older cottages looked almost as if they had grown naturally from the land.

In the main, countryfolk were dependent on the land for their living in the nineteenth century. William Howitt, in his tours of England that produced the various editions of *The Rural Life of England* in the 1830s and 1840s, observed the differences between one part of the country and another, and the type of work that was to be found in each locality: 'The ploughman whistling after his team; the shepherds on the downs, driving their white flocks before them like a rolling cloud to evening fold or morning pasture; the dwellers on heaths and moors, paring the turf for fuel, or cutting from the peat-beds their black bricks, and piling their black pyramids on the waste... Each district has its peculiar pursuit and occupation pointed out by nature, and all these things give variety to the country and its inhabitants.'

There were villages watched over by the family in the 'big house', or by a clergyman eager to carry out his duty, assisted by a conscientious wife. In others, resident authority of this kind, to direct the lives of the villagers, was lacking. 'Every village,' wrote Thomas Hardy, 'has its idiosyncrasy, its constitution.'

In some parts of England, the buildings of a village are grouped around the church and parsonage, with knots of cottages and houses. This arrangement is common in the south and the

The villages of Moreton Pinkney, Northamptonshire (below), and Godshill on the Isle of Wight (below right), both had a deep muddy street winding through the village, worn down by generations of wheeled carts and feet, and lined by a picturesque jumble of thatched and tiled cottages.

Midlands; elsewhere, and especially in upland regions, rural settlement is scattered, comprising hamlets or a sprinkling of individual farmsteads. Many of these places were formed by clearing away woodland and building in the clearings. Lanes circle woods that have long since been felled, and cottages surround greens that were once in the middle of woodland. The village green may be the only remnant of the common land that the village once had, on which there were rights to graze animals and gather wood, and where festivities were held.

Then there are villages like The Bourne, on the edge of Farnham in Surrey, which was a squatters' village. There people had built themselves small houses on land nobody else claimed or owned. George Sturt wrote of it: 'As you look down the valley from its high sides, hardly anywhere are there to be seen three cottages in a row, but all about the steep slopes the little mean dwelling-places are scattered in disorder. So it extends east and west for perhaps a mile and a half – a surprisingly populous hollow...' All over England there were little irregular villages of this kind that had mushroomed in the early decades of the last century. The name of the Wiltshire village of Nomansland reveals its origins; and Juniper Hill, Lark Rise in Flora Thompson's *Lark Rise to Candleford*, is described as 'the spot God made with the left-overs when He'd finished creating the rest of the earth.'

A girl buys cherries from an itinerant trader. With few shops in the village, families depended on hawkers for fruit that was not grown locally, fish and other foods as well as for household wares. The painting is by William Collins.

A row of old cottages at Sutton Scotney, Hampshire, painted by Isobel Naftel in 1886. The villagers' gardens, where they would grow potatoes and other vegetables as well as a few flowers, are across the street.

From that Oxfordshire village, Flora Thompson occasionally passed through that other quintessentially Victorian type of village: the estate village. She remembered it vividly: all was neat and tidy, with orderly rows of roomy cottages, a pump for each small group of houses, and everyone at church (it being a Sunday). Only good people lived there, her father had told her. Many Victorian landowners and philanthropists built model dwellings in model villages on their estates, bringing in architects to design cottages for the labourers, almshouses for the aged poor, and often a show-piece home farm to demonstrate the latest trends in agricultural

techniques to the tenantry and to visitors. With a planned layout, and uniform materials with identical architectural detailing, the estate village was the most highly developed type of rural settlement in Victorian England.

New in the nineteenth century were the purpose-built schools, as charitable efforts and then national compulsory schemes brought education to every corner of the land. Many villages still have the high classrooms, the enclosed playground, and the separate boys' and girls' entrances of their Victorian schools, where rows of children with their slates were taught the rudiments of reading, 'riting and 'rithmetic.

With these new elements, a Victorian village often contained relics from its past. The village cross – a broken shaft approached by a few steps, perhaps – might be the only vestige of the market which had once been held there. A medieval preaching cross might still stand. The pound, or pinfold, might survive, where cattle that had been found wandering at night were kept until claimed by their owner.

The human equivalent to the pound was the lock-up, where a man who had stayed too long at the alehouse might be kept overnight. As the parish constable was replaced by the village bobby,

Whipping post and stocks, still standing on many a village green, are reminders of an earlier, crueller time well within the living memory of many Victorian villagers.

The butcher's shop, from P. F. Robinson's Village Architecture. *Depending on the size and prosperity of the village, it might also boast a general store, a chandler and a beer shop.*

with his handcuffs and police cells, so the lock-up ceased to be needed. There might be other reminders of ancient punishment, such as the stocks, or a public whipping post for the public humiliation of offenders. The stocks at Ninfield, in East Sussex, are made of iron, an unusual relic of the local Wealden iron industry.

Most country areas had no mains water supply, so the parish pump or well was the principal source of water. To the women of the village, the pump or well was what the inn was to the men; a place to gather and discuss the small-scale news of the day.

'Farewell, then, my beloved village,' wrote Miss Mitford at the end of *Our Village*, 'the long straggling street, gay and bright in this sunny, windy April morning, full of all implements of dirt and noise – men, women, children, cows, horses, wagons, carts, pigs, dogs, geese, and chickens, busy, merry, stirring little world, farewell! Farewell to the winding uphill road, with its clouds of dust as horsemen and carriages ascend the gentle eminence, its borders of turf, and its primrosy hedgerows! – Farewell to the breezy common, with its islands of cottages and cottage gardens... its cricket-ground where children already linger anticipating their summer revelry; its pretty boundary of field and woodland, and distant farms.'

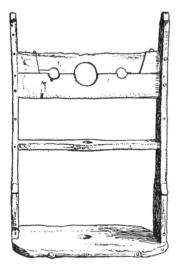

The pillory, formerly set up in every market place for the punishment of swindlers, liars and cheats, had been replaced early in the nineteenth century by fines and imprisonment.

The almshouses, also from Village Architecture, built by leading families of the neighbourhood, were charitable foundations for the poor and indigent of the village. In some cases they dated back to the sixteenth and seventeenth centuries.

THE PARISH CHURCH

The parish church at Whittlesford, near Cambridge, by Richard Bankes Harraden. The churchyard was a valuable open space in the village.

'I HAVE RARELY SEEN Langley [Burrell] Church and Church-yard look more beautiful than they did this morning. The weather was lovely and round the quiet Church the trees were gorgeous, the elms dazzling golden and the beeches burning crimson... The place lay quiet in the still autumn sun-shine. Then the latch of the wicket gate tinkled and pretty Keren Wood appeared coming along the Church path under the spreading boughs of the wide larch, and in the glare of yellow light the bell broke solemnly through the golden elms that stood stately round the Church.' This was the scene that greeted the Reverend Francis Kilvert one October morn-ing in the 1870s.

The parish church is one of the traditional focuses of the village, its walls surrounding the assembled population at prayer, its interior and graveyard holding the memorials and the mortal remains of erstwhile parishioners. This was the setting for the weekly and yearly round of the Church of England, and for many parochial activities, too.

The appearance of most village churches today owes something to the Victorians, who swept away the fittings of their Georgian predecessors. The two sides of Anglicanism, the fervour of the Evangelicals, and the ritualistic revival associated with the High Church of the Oxford Movement, both promoted change. Eighteenth-century box pews were abolished and replaced by rows of bench pews, facing an altar with a decorative frontal and altar cloth, instead of a plain table covered with a linen cloth. Encaustic 'medieval' tiles took the place of stone flags underfoot, and brightly coloured stained glass appeared in the windows. A choir, robed and in the chancel, and an organ replaced the rustic music-making of local players in the gallery at the west end.

(Right) The village choir, painted by Thomas Webster. The choir and congregation are wearing their Sunday best. The instrumentalists, the 'cello, bassoon and oboe players, would be replaced by an organ or harmonium later in the century.

The choir in Thomas Hardy's *A Few Crusted Characters* were able to 'turn a jig or a hornpipe out of hand as well as ever they could turn out a psalm, and perhaps better'. But rustic musicians did not accord with the more respectable tone of the mid-Victorians. The players in *A Few Crusted Characters* became intoxicated during the service and broke into dance tunes, urging the congregation 'every man kiss his pardner under the mistletoe'. The barrel organ that replaced them 'would play two and twenty new psalm tunes', and it had 'a really respectable man to turn the winch'. Village orchestras soon became a dim memory.

The clergy of Victorian England were not, perhaps, as closely identified with the gentry as they had been in the eighteenth century, when the 'squarson' (squire and parson combined) was a familiar figure. The social standing of the Victorian country clergyman was none the less high. The rectory or vicarage would often be the largest house in the village if there were no resident squire (and sometimes even if there was). Many clergy were directly appointed to their benefices by the local landowners, and they had an essential stake in the produce of the land through the ever-contentious tithe in those areas where it applied. A clergyman in Hardy's story, *A Tragedy of Two Ambitions*, summed up the position: 'To succeed in the Church, people must believe in you,

The ancient tiled lych-gate of Beckenham churchyard. At a funeral the bier was set down beneath the gateway to await the clergyman's arrival. This momentary pause symbolized the transition from life to death.

first of all, as a gentleman, secondly as a man of means, thirdly as a scholar, fourthly as a preacher, fifthly, perhaps, as a Christian.'

In the 1890s Alison Uttley (calling herself Susan Garland, as the author of *The Country Child*) would go to church with her mother. Village society sat in church, ordered by rank: 'Behind Sir Harry Vane sat two pews full of maids, demurely dressed in black, with small neat bonnets on their parted hair. They hurried out of church before the family, like a company of mice before a cat. Sir Harry Vane, as the Squire, the owner of many farms and most of the villages and land, had the right to turn round in church and to go up first at Holy Communion. Susan's glance never ventured higher than his gold watch-chain and seals.

'There was Mrs Stone, the vicar's wife, in a dress of mauve silk... There were the girls from Dial Grange... They walked out with their governess, each carrying twin prayer and hymn books in red morocco cases.

'Then came Sir Harry's housekeeper, a stout comfortable woman with a high bosom. She walked slowly and sedately as befitted her rank.'

Dissenting congregations, such as the Baptists and Methodists, which established a very firm hold in some parts of the country, behaved differently. The contrast between Church and Chapel was drawn by one observer at the end of Victoria's reign. The squire, his tenants and estate employees, were all there in church: 'And with these must be numbered a sprinkling of the very poor, who hobble up the aisle, making a fine show of rheumatic pains and not forgetting the prospect of Christmas coals. In the chapel gather "ungenteel" farmers, usually the smaller tenants, artisans, and shopkeepers, with a sprinkling of "free" labourers and farm servants. The congregation taken in the bulk is worth much less money than in the parish church, and the dissenting parson is in many ways the same as his hearers. "Oh, we don't mind the minister, he is just like one of ourselves," the cottager will say.'

Villagers went to church for the ceremonies of baptism and marriage, and for the burial of the dead. The parish registers recorded the generations passing through. Death was all around, for more than one child in ten would die before his or her first birthday, to be laid to rest along with all the previous generations of villagers in the churchyard.

A church in Sussex, near Hastings. The tumbledown state of many of England's parish churches would receive the attention of restorers during the course of the century.

The west end of a church with children assembled on the staircase leading to the musicians' gallery, a watercolour by W. H. Hunt. The interior of the Gothic church is as it would have been at the beginning of Queen Victoria's reign.

VILLAGE CHARACTERS

Every Victorian village had its characters – the gossip, the boaster, the ne'er-do-well, the idiot, the hero, the never-grumbling, the always-grumbling. In such a small and close-knit community, every foible and eccentricity was known and discussed, every particularity of feature or expression drew comment.

The blacksmith's forge, especially if it were situated close to a public house, was a regular place for gossip. It was often here that the stories concerning the more colourful or outspoken villagers originated and were circulated, for it was a place of resort for idlers, at least according to the Reverend Richard Cobbold, rector of Wortham in Suffolk.

In the imagination, colourful characters tend to become larger than life, but Cobbold's descriptions, and the portraits he painted of his parishioners in the 1860s, are true to life: 'George Minter is beyond all doubt the scamp of the country. He has been sent to gaol twelve times for refusing to work and for vagabondism, and yet no reformation takes place in the man.

'"My philosophy is this – Be content. I never was otherwise," said the offender.'

The village shop often seemed to produce characters who endured in the popular memory. The shop was 'a repository for bread, shoes, tea, cheese, tape, ribands, and bacon; for everything, in short, except the one particular thing which you happen to want at the moment'. Cobbold recorded: 'The Village Shop! Who in the parish of Wortham can forget Mr Browne or Mr Browne's shop? Here all the villagers go to post their letters for the Post Office is here established! Here also, the paupers of the parish go to receive the liberal dole of the Poor Laws... Independent, then of all the private considerations of each person's traffic, from actual necessity – the public accommodation of the Post Office and Relieving Officer's duty – would render Mr Browne's Shop a place to be much observed.'

The Victorian village postman, depicted by William Hemsley. A young woman detains the postman on his round and waits eagerly to see if he has the hoped-for letter. The new penny post, introduced in 1840, made the postage of letters affordable to all.

The postman, too, was one of the local characters, a familiar figure on his daily round of the cottages and farms. In another village, in addition to serving as universal provider, the shopkeeper acted as sexton and parish clerk, and owned a cart drawn by a broken-winded pony that could be hired for slow journeys. Cobbold tells how Old Israel Garnham ran Wortham's main mode of transport, with his donkeys and cart: 'He and his donkeys were constant features in the parish. He then took it into his head that there was more to be got by industry in America than in England. So without saying a word to any of his friends he quietly marches off, gets a passage to America, works his way over – and finds that sharper fellows than himself do not succeed there better than they do here. So home he comes again – walks into his house – and takes to work with his donkeys and his cart just as if he had only been to see his brother in the shires.'

The poacher was frequently the village hero. 'If I had been born an idiot,' wrote James Hawker in a diary of his life in Victorian Leicestershire, 'and unfit to carry a gun – though with plenty of cash – they would have called me a grand sportsman. Being born poor, I am called a poacher.'

There were 'mouchers', who loitered along the roads and hedges, picking up whatever they could, but the real poacher was, in Richard Jefferies' words, a 'shrewd fellow, with a power of silence, capable of delicacy of touch which almost raises poaching into a fine art'. He was 'often a sober and to all appearances industrious individual, working steadily during the day at some handicraft in the village, as blacksmithing, hedge-carpentering. . . cobbling, tinkering, or perhaps in the mill; a somewhat reserved, solitary workman of superior intelligence and frequently advanced views as to the "rights of labour".'

Hawker was a true countryman, who knew and followed all the animals in the woods and loved to spend the nights with the landlord's property to himself. Poaching was an adventure, a thrilling deception of the gamekeeper and of the pheasants and partridges, the rabbits and hares that were his quarry.

Others classed as heroes were the sporting men who brought fame to the village: the high-scoring batsmen and the champion wrestlers. Abraham Cann, the giant of Dartmoor, was a wrestler of national renown, whose impressive appearance and rude skill

Characters from the Reverend Richard Cobbold's village of Wortham, Suffolk, painted and described by him in 1860.

(Top) Rebecca Bobby, mother of a large family and a widow, who kept the dame school. 'She was however very ignorant herself and like many who teach young children was imposing rather than enlightening.'

(Centre) Ann Smith, known as 'Old Doody', wife of Harry Smith the village blacksmith. 'She was always constant to her work and constant to her Church,' to the gratification of Cobbold.

(Bottom) Sarah Goddard, who lived to the age of eighty-three and whose maxim was, 'When you don't feel well resolve not to eat or drink anything for twenty-four hours, and you will feel yourself wonderfully better the next day.' She was her own savings bank and steward as well as her own doctor.

(Top) *Charles Y. Browne, keeper of the Wortham village shop, which was also the post office. He was described by Cobbold as 'ready for an argument any time' and as 'one of the craniologists, phrenologists, or free thinking men, who maintain that according to physical construction so will be the outward and inward man.'*

(Centre) *George Minter, not a bad-looking man when shaved and properly dressed in Cobbold's opinion, was 'the scamp of the country', sent to gaol twelve times for 'refusing to work and for vagabondism'. He rated himself a philosopher and spoke 'in the pompous language of the theatre'.*

(Bottom) *George Howlett, the Wortham village schoolmaster. He was 'a specimen of a gone by day – when the Fear of God was taught together with a competent degree of arithmetic, writing and reading – but the intricacies of science were not then taught with their A.B.C.'*

were reported in the *London Magazine*. When William Howitt was collecting material for his book on the rural life of England, Polkinhorne of St Columb, an innkeeper, had become the acknowledged champion of the West, and he encountered the defeated Cann selling halfpenny tickets on the footbridge between Plymouth and Devonport.

The schoolteacher was commonly the most ridiculed person in the village. At Wortham, George Howlett 'was a specimen of a gone by day' and describing Maria Jolly, who ran the Dame School, Cobbold wrote: 'She required no puffing up from others, being sufficiently puffed up within herself to think herself wonderfully clever... and in one sense she was! – because anyone may teach that they do understand, but it requires a very clever person to teach that they do not understand!' Little wonder then that he found the cunning of his parishioners more admirable than their scholastic attainment.

By no means every village had a doctor, and a local person with a modicum of medical knowledge would take on the role. In Miss Mitford's village, their 'doctor' was 'neither physician, nor surgeon, nor apothecary', though uniting the offices of all three, 'an oracle, and always (with reverence be it spoken) a quack'. Some villages had the sort of quaint quack that Richard Heath came across in Surrey in the 1870s. His sign board read:

Worm Doctor
Professor Medical Botany
Herb Medicines prepared for every complaint
Advice Gratis

'The owner thereof was a shrewd, taciturn old man . . . a believer in the wonderful potency of herbs, and had scraped together such knowledge as a shrewd man, who had lived in various countries, must have many opportunities of acquiring.' Often there was a 'wise woman' of the village, but in many country areas there were still fears about witchcraft.

Last but not least was the hereditary eccentricity of some of the landowning families: squires such as Jack Mytton, of Halston in Shropshire, who, to entertain his guests, once appeared in the drawing-room in hunting dress riding a bear and set himself on fire to get rid of a fit of hiccups.

THE BIG HOUSE

'**I**T IS A COMFORTABLE FEELING to know you stand on your own ground. Land is about the only thing that can't fly away. And then, you see, land gives so much more than the rent. It gives position and influence and political power, to say nothing of the game.' Such was the opinion of Anthony Trollope's Archdeacon Grantly. The truth about land was revealed to the nation in 1872, when the only systematic survey of land ownership since the Domesday Book was conducted. Almost a million people owned land in England and Wales, yet 7,000 people owned four-fifths of the total acreage. In England there were 1,363 large landowners (with more than 1,000 acres), who between them owned almost half of the country. In some parts, like the East Riding of Yorkshire and Rutland, almost all the land belonged to a great estate. In other areas, however, there were few estates – in counties such as Essex, Kent, Surrey, Leicestershire and Cambridgeshire, where smaller farmers who owned their own land were common.

In Flora Thompson's little hamlet of Lark Rise, there was no local big house, and the gentry, who occasionally passed by, 'flitted across the scene like kingfishers crossing a flock of hedgerow sparrows'. Elsewhere, the great and the wealthy – and their houses – dominated village life. Considerable new wealth was generated by Victorian heavy industry or in trade, banking and the professions, which usually found its way into land. The new rich either bought and set themselves up on an existing estate, or had the daunting task of building one up from scratch.

The Georgian ideal had been to build a country house within parkland which extended in all directions, but excluded the villagers. Sometimes whole villages were swept away, and rebuilt out of sight, to make way for a rolling park. By contrast, the Victorian ideal was to include the villagers and their cottages as part of the grand design, as was made clear in the influential writings of John Claudius Loudon. 'To me,' he wrote in 1853, 'nothing is more

On a fine day in May 1834, Lord Egremont entertained more than 4,000 of the poor of the neighbourhood on the lawn in front of Petworth House, the subject of William Frederick Witherington's painting. 'Two great tents were erected in the middle to receive the provisions, which were conveyed in carts like ammunition,' wrote Charles Greville. 'Plum puddings and loaves were piled like cannon balls, and innumerable joints of boiled and roast beef were spread out.'

cheerless than that exclusive solitary grandeur so much affected in the present day, which forbids the poor even to set foot within the precincts of greatness. As the most beautiful landscape is incomplete without figures, so the general effect of a park is always lonely, unless it have a footpath frequented by the picturesque figures of the labouring classes, and giving life and interest to the scene.' The villagers might be permitted access, but they should still be left in no doubt of their place.

Tennyson gave all the qualities of a Victorian country gentleman to Sir Walter Vivian in 'The Princess':

> No little lily-handed Baronet he,
> A great broad-shouldered genial Englishman,
> A lord of fat prize-oxen and of sheep,
> A raiser of huge melons and of pine.
>
> A patron of some thirty charities,
> A pamphleteer on guano and on grain,
> A quarter-sessions chairman, abler none;
> Fair-hair'd and redder than a windy morn.

One of his real-life counterparts, the fifteenth Earl of Derby, set out his creed, describing the responsibilities of a great landowner: 'The objects which men aim at when they become possessed of land may I think be enumerated as follows: political influence; social importance, founded on territorial possession, the most visible and unmistakable form of wealth; power exercised over tenantry; the pleasure of managing, directing, and improving the estate itself; residential enjoyment, including what is called sport;

'Cottage dwellings in various styles', designs offered by J. C. Loudon in his 1857 edition of Encyclopedia of Cottage, Farm and Villa Architecture *and suitable for a gentleman's estate. Housing for the labourers and estate workers was intended to blend harmoniously with the landscape.*

(Below) *'A cottage dwelling in the Old English style.'*

A picturesque four-roomed cottage (centre) with 'a rustic verandah along one front, constructed of barked oak branches, on which vines and other flowering shrubs are twined'.

A castellated lodge (below), described as suitable for a gardener or other upper servant.

the money return – the rent.' It had become an axiom of Victorian society that possession of an estate carried with it as many responsibilities as rewards. Lady Bracknell, in Oscar Wilde's *The Importance of Being Earnest*, with humour that contained much truth, declared: 'What between the duties expected of one during one's lifetime, and the duties extracted from one after one's death, land has ceased to be either a profit or a pleasure. It gives one position, and prevents one from keeping it up.' That was written in 1895, when agriculture was depressed and the heyday of the Victorian landed estate had passed.

Sir George Gilbert Scott believed that the responsibility of the landed proprietor should be expressed in his house as well as in his demeanour: 'He has been placed by Providence in a position of authority and dignity, and no false modesty should deter him from expressing this, quietly and gravely, in the character of his house.' Scott was the architect of several country houses including Kelham Hall, near Newark in Nottinghamshire, built in hard, red brick. This was a house fulfilling his mission to prove that a building with modern conveniences and good lighting could be contained in a muscular Gothic style. From its imposing frontage, John Henry Manners-Sutton could look across the River Trent to the land he owned beyond. Up to the 1860s, the Gothic style was adopted by old landowning families such as the Manners-Suttons as well as by new wealth such as the Gibbs family, who made their fortune in the Peruvian guano trade. The latter had John Norton build them a grand Gothic house at Tyntesfield near Bristol. It was much admired by Charlotte M. Yonge, a family friend: 'That beautiful house was like a church in spirit.'

Loudon suggested that the tiles used for cladding this cottage (below) be old ones to avoid 'the glaring hue' of those fresh from the kiln.

The single-storey thatched cottage (centre), 'comfortable and commodious', had the option of wash-house, chicken coop, pigsty, dirt-bin and wood-house. It is difficult to judge how many Victorian landowners would have provided their employees with such improved housing.

The cottage (below) described as being in the 'Old English Manner', included a dairy, cow-house, pigsty and a place for hay and straw.

A big house, J. C. Loudon thought, 'should always form part of a village, and be placed, if possible, on rather higher ground, that it may appear to be a sort of head and protector of the surrounding dwellings of the poor'. The building of model dwellings for villagers became an important part of the improvement of a mid-Victorian landed estate. One little girl, whose father unexpectedly inherited an estate at Presteigne on the Welsh border in 1861, recorded the changes that were made: 'After completing the manor and the grounds, he determined to build a new vicarage, church, and cottages for his labourers. The vicarage was soon built and the new cottages which [were] made very comfortable and were in a row by the side of the road as you drove through the village. . . So Norton became a pattern village and very proud and very happy we were of all that our dear father had done, and how he had made himself beloved by all in the parish and on the estate.'

A great hall was often incorporated into the designs for a new country house: the place where the tenants would receive hospitality in medieval style. The farmers would be entertained in the great hall; the local gentry in the dining-room. At Petworth in 1834 the labouring families feasted at tables set up on the lawn.

One of the lasting features of the relationship of the family in the big house with their tenants and poorer neighbours was the philanthropy of the ladies, performing the role of 'Lady Bountiful'. The elderly and poor families in the villages were visited and given food, clothing and financial assistance as well as helpful advice. Charitable help was given in the knowledge that this was the right thing to do; on the whole it was received with a display of gratitude and deference. The labouring poor had benefit clubs, clothing, coal and shoe clubs, subscribed to and chiefly supported by their employers; dinners and treats were given at Christmas and harvest; schools for the children were kept up at the expense of their employers and landlords. As one Suffolk lady wrote: 'All these are benefits and comforts which are not thought of, and would not be feasible in large manufacturing districts, but which add materially to the happiness and unity of the two classes – employers and labourers.'

Then there was the opportunity for employment that a great house could offer to men and women of all ages living in the surrounding area. Dozens of local people might be employed in

Charity, personified by the gentlewoman who arrives with her exquisitely dressed and ringletted daughter to visit a sick village child. An oil painting by Thomas Brooks of 1860. The contrast between the hothouse grapes arranged in a basket and the half-peeled turnip lying on the floor of the cottage is one of several in the picture.

house, stables, garden or on the estate, and a place in service there was often a first job which, for a woman in particular, might lead in due course to a move to the city.

Quite small country houses would have a complement of eight servants, while the largest establishments had forty or more. The servants were divided into strict categories, above and below stairs. *The Gentleman's House* of 1864, the classic planning manual, divided a country house into nine sections: Kitchen Offices, Upper Servants' Offices, Lower Servants' Offices, Laundry Offices, Bakery and Brewery, Cellars and Storage, Servants' Private Rooms, Supplementaries and Thoroughfares. Robert Kerr, the author of the manual, paid particular attention to the kitchens, which often had a separate wing to themselves. This could mean long walks for the servants, especially when as in many large households meals might be served in the dining-room, the nursery, the school-room, and the servants' hall.

An occasion that involved the outdoor as well as the indoor servants was the shooting party. The house and grounds were prepared with the utmost attention to detail, sometimes with the assistance of extra help from the village; local men and boys were recruited as beaters. Gamekeepers were ceaselessly waging war against poachers, protecting the game that they raised. Until the progressive repeal of the Game Laws, which had made the shooting (and even the sale) of game an exclusively landowning

The joint authors of the 'Shooting' volume of the Badminton Library series, Lord Walsingham and Sir Ralph Payne-Gallwey, Bt, illustrated the correct form for the sportsman and his loader to change guns.

privilege, the pursuit of birds, hares, rabbits and the like was one of the most socially divisive of all rural issues. Village people would often feel that they had a right to any birds and beasts they could catch in the woods and fields, and the poacher was frequently something of a local hero.

By the end of the nineteenth century, when the pheasant had become the principal quarry, the shooting party was expected to secure large bags. At Holkham Hall in north Norfolk, for example, 3,000 game birds would have been shot in a year at the end of the eighteenth century. By 1880, 3,000 might be shot on a single good day.

Where a big house was part of the rural scene, its influence was widely felt. The owners of land in Victorian times helped to create the type of village now regarded as the essence of rural life.

Hundreds of pheasants were reared by the gamekeeper. The Badminton Library series declared that 'one of the chief attractions of true sport' for the gun was 'the satisfaction of feeling that his knowledge of the habits of the game and the manner in which it can best be approached, has enabled him to reduce into possession, in a sportsmanlike fashion, a goodly proportion of whatever numbers may have been available.'

The success of the shoot depended on the number of birds that the gamekeeper and his men could produce on the day. They would be tipped sovereigns and half-sovereigns by the shooting-party guests.

COTTAGE INTERIORS

'THERE IS HIS TENEMENT of, at most, one or two rooms. His naked wall; bare brick, stone, or mud floor, as it may be; a few wooden or rush-bottomed chairs; a deal or old oak table; a simple fireplace with its oven beside it, or, in many parts of the kingdom, no other fireplace than the hearth; a few pots and pans – and you have his whole abode, goods and chattels. He comes home weary from his out-door work, having eaten his dinner under hedge or tree, and seats himself for a few hours with his wife and children, then turns into a rude bed, standing perhaps on the farther side of his only room, and out again before daylight, if it be winter ...

A late Victorian cottage home, painted by William Snape. The furnishing of the cottage is sparse, but the interior is enlivened by the geraniums on the windowsill. On the walls are a calendar from The Churchman's Almanack *and a portrait of the widowed Queen Victoria taken from an illustrated magazine.*

Carlton A. Smith's 'First Steps'. The labourer with his clay pipe watches his daughter and young grandchild. The bed was one of the principal pieces of furniture and candles or rushlights the only type of lighting until the 1860s, when paraffin lamps began to be used in the cottages.

'In this little hut, which we should hardly think would do for a cowshed or a hayloft, and to which the stables of many gentlemen are real palaces, is the poor man packed with all his kindred lives, interests, and affections...' So wrote William Howitt of a typical country cottage of the 1840s.

Nearly forty years later, Richard Jefferies described broadly similar conditions still existing in a cottage in the West Country: 'It consists of two rooms, oblong, and generally of the same size – one to live in, the other to sleep in... At one end there is a small shed for odds and ends. This shed used to be built with an oven, but now scarcely any labourers bake their own bread, but buy of the baker... The floor consists simply of the earth itself rammed down hard, or sometimes of rough pitching-stones, with large interstices in between them. The furniture of this room is of the simplest description. A few chairs, a deal table, three or four shelves, and a cupboard, with a box or two in the corners, constitute the whole. The domestic utensils are equally few, and strictly utilitarian. A great pot, a kettle, a saucepan, a few plates, dishes and knives, half-a-dozen spoons, and that is about all. But on the mantelpiece there is nearly sure to be a few ornaments in crockery, bought from some itinerant trader.' Jefferies might also have mentioned spoon racks and boxes for salt and herbs, and that the hanging shelves were to keep food out of the reach of vermin.

Larger dwellings were on two floors, joined merely by a ladder in the oldest and most primitive. The windows in the bedrooms were low and tucked right under the eaves, and it was only possible to stand upright in the centre of the rooms. The simplest cottages had bare rafters overhead, with no plaster ceiling.

Almost all cottages, however simple and scantily furnished, were maintained with care to give them an air of decency. And not all the rooms were as bleak as those that served as living-room and kitchen described by Howitt and Jefferies. Some had dressers laden with crockery, cushions on the chairs and brightly coloured hand-made rag rugs on the floor. In the older cottages there might be a grandfather clock, a gate-legged table and a row of pewter vessels from a time when life was easier for country folk.

'Dressers are fixtures essential to every kitchen, but more especially to that of the cottager, to whom they serve both as dressers and sideboards', and it was intended that large heavy pots would be placed under the drawers. So wrote J. C. Loudon beside this illustration in his Encyclopedia of Cottage, Farm and Villa Architecture of 1857.

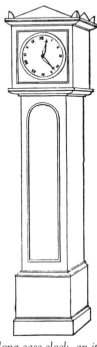

A long-case clock, an item for better-off cottage homes. The oak case could have been made by the village joiner, but the clock movement would have come from the local town.

Two chair designs from Loudon's Encyclopedia: (top) a Windsor chair which he describes as popular in the Midlands and made of elm and (above) a 'comfortable and cheap chair' which if not painted could be stained with diluted sulphuric acid and logwood to give the effect of mahogany.

Jefferies described a cottage with walls completely covered with engravings from the *Illustrated London News* as decoration. In the more comfortable dwellings, there would sometimes be a Staffordshire pottery figure, one of the tens of thousands that were manufactured commemorating some great figure of the century or personifying a virtue. Cheaper ornaments were the china 'fairings' bought at the fairs. There might also be a picture of Queen Victoria taken from a pictorial paper. The coming of photography, which by the 1860s was within the grasp of any family with a few spare pence in the local market town, also meant that a family, however poor, might have acquired a portrait or two.

At the heart of every cottage was the hearth, around which all the family clustered for warmth and comfort, and before which the woman spent much of her time. In the early part of Queen Victoria's reign, most of the cooking was done in an iron pot suspended from a hook over the open wood or peat fire; from the hook was also hung the occasional joint of meat for roasting. Faggots, collected in the woods and from along the lanes, were quickly consumed by the fire that was kept alight all the time.

Cast-iron kitchen ranges, capable of supplying all the heat required, not only for cooking, but also for washing, warming, and every other domestic purpose, were usually installed by landlords rather than the cottagers themselves, and they did not become standard fixtures until the 1880s. By then, the railways had brought coal, at a reasonable price, to places remote from where it had been mined. The ranges were developed from the hob grates that had plates on either side providing a hot surface for boiling kettles and heating flat irons. At first, the fire was open to the chimney, and pots and joints were still suspended on a hook or chain above or in front of the flames. To one side of a traditional range was an oven, and to the other a boiler for water, fitted with a tap on the later models.

As well as the utensils used for cooking, the cottage kitchen would contain various bowls and pails made by the local turner or cooper. Some of the women would take in washing – for the big house or the rectory – and for this and their own linen and clothes they

Loudon's illustration for a settle: 'the back forms an excellent screen or protection from the current of air which is continually passing from door to chimney... in a superior kind of cottage the back of the settle might be ornamented with prints or maps in the manner of a screen.'

would need large wooden tubs or troughs and a rubbing board. With the tall barrel-like tubs they would use a 'dolly' on a stem to swirl the washing around in the water, or a 'peggy', which was a form of plunger. These stood in a corner of the room when they were not being used.

The washing was done on a Monday or Tuesday so that clothes were ironed and ready to put on clean on Sunday. The water was boiled in large copper vessels, often in the same pot that was used for steaming suet puddings and cooking stews. In summer, when it was fine, the washing was done out of doors, with a fire specially lit to heat the water. A hedgerow made a convenient washing line.

Jefferies complained of the smell that arose from the cottages, which he found to be particularly offensive when coming from 'the fresh air of the fields, perhaps from the sweet scent of clover or of new-mown grass'. In a cottage: 'The floor may be scrubbed, the walls brushed, the chairs clean, and the beds tidy; it is from outside that all the noisome exhalations taint the breeze. The refuse, vegetables, the washings, the liquid and solid rubbish generally is cast out into the ditch, and there festers till the first storm sweeps it away. The cleanest woman indoors thinks nothing disgusting out of doors, and hardly goes a step from her threshold to cast away filth.'

Rush lights, which were the most primitive form of lighting, were still in use in cottages well into the nineteenth century. The rushes, collected in late summer or autumn, were peeled and then, according to William Cobbett, mutton grease 'is melted and put into something as long as the rushes are. The rushes are put into the grease, soaked in it sufficiently, then taken out and laid in a bit of bark taken from a young tree.' Cobbett regarded candles as unsuitable for cottage dwellings, but certainly any woman doing close work such as lace-making would need the rather stronger light that they gave out. Spinning, sewing and mending were often done by the light of the fire, but the spinning wheel was normally positioned close to the window for daytime work. Window seats were created in the thickness of the wall so that the cottagers could take advantage of the daylight coming through the leaded lights, but many preferred to do their work on the doorstep or in the back yard. Because of the small size of the rooms and the darkness of the interiors, children played mainly out of doors.

In a painting by William Henry Midwood of 1873, a countryman displays his favourite flowers. Cottagers grew auricula, polyanthus, pinks and geraniums in pots on sunny windowsills with a view to entering them in flower shows. At these, prizes such as copper kettles, silver teaspoons and brass candlesticks, as seen on the mantelpiece, were awarded. The object placed to one side of the hearth is a skein-winder for wool.

Paraffin lamps were introduced into cottage homes from the 1860s and the very much brighter light obtained from them fundamentally altered the pattern of existence. The working day, especially for women at home, was extended by several hours since paraffin was comparatively cheap, as were the brass, china and glass lamps.

At first, there were fears about the safety of paraffin, and the elderly were of course the last to change to the newer type of lighting. Life was always hard for the elderly and housebound. When Francis Kilvert went to visit one of his oldest parishioners, Sally Killing, in 1873: 'She asked me the usual and indeed invariable question whether I remembered her old thatched cottage, near the road, by the lilac bush, and the old house in Westfield. I asked her how she passed her time. "Aw ther," she said, "I do rock and sway myself about."'

The reports from the nineteenth century in general show that people found what they hoped to inside village houses, whether it be order and care, the profligacy of the poor, or the terrible conditions landowners inflicted upon their tenants. Thomas Hardy, in his essay on the Dorset labourer, wrote that nothing was more common than for some philanthropic lady to burst in upon a family, and be struck by the apparent squalor of the scene. He was credibly informed that the impression received depended on whether there were bright colours in the cottage, apparently indicating a clean and happy home – and that appearances might deceive. Cosy cottage domesticity was easier to achieve in summer than in winter, when a mud floor would be damp and sticky, and the draught only one degree better than the smoke. There was more than enough fresh air through the keyhole.

Richard Health, while condemning living conditions in some parts of England, was disposed to find them better in the north, even in winter. In one cottage that he visited, 'The mahogany furniture, bright with hand-polish, the display of crockery and ornaments, the easy comfort of every arrangement, seen in the dancing light of a brilliant coal-fire, all tell of good housewifery and ample incomes. Every fireplace, too, has its set-pot and oven, both being in constant requi-

A stewpot and kettle suspended from ratchet hangers over a wood fire in a cottage at Garnacott in North Devon at the end of the nineteenth century.

sition, for they have plenty of meat. Yet the good wife will tell you that they had a "sair" fight for it before the children earned anything . . . On a winter's evening the family circle gather round the cheerful fire, the women knitting, the father mending shoes – an art nearly all acquire – while one of the younger ones reads for the benefit of the whole group.'

By the end of the nineteenth century, traditional cottage life was disappearing. The inconveniences of living in dwellings with mud, or even cold stone and brick floors, with the most basic forms of lighting and heating, were being overcome just as the villages were being deserted by their inhabitants in favour of the towns. Eight years after Queen Victoria died, there existed a strong feeling of nostalgia for the simple cottages, and Stewart Dick wrote in a book of Helen Allingham's paintings, 'houses live longer than men, and change with the times less rapidly. The same roof serves as a covering for many generations, and if one were asked what is the most typical thing in England, one would reply at once, the old English cottage.'

Three generations of villagers inside a cottage. Stairs and a ladder lead to an upper floor, where most of the family would sleep, and a bed in the wall of the living-room is reached by a rope ladder.

COTTAGE GARDENS

'ONE END OF THE COTTAGE is often completely hidden with ivy, and woodbine grows in thickest profusion over the porch. Near the door there are almost always a few cabbage rose trees, and under the windows grow wall-flowers and hollyhocks, sweet peas, columbine, and sometimes the graceful lilies of the valley. The garden stretches in a long strip from the door, one mass of green. It is enclosed by thick hedges, over which the dog-rose grows, and the wild convolvulus will flower in the autumn. Trees fill up every available space and corner – apple trees, pear trees, damsons, plums, bullaces – all varieties . . . In odd corners there are sure to be a few specimens of southernwood, mugwort and other herbs.'

Richard Jefferies wrote this description of the English cottage garden in a collection of essays, *The Toilers of the Field*. With its profusion of old varieties of flowers, herbs, vegetables and fruit,

'Hot Afternoon' by Alfred Parsons. A dog sleeps in the heat by a ramshackle fence, on which a crow sits, in contrast to its caged cousin. The front garden is a riot of late summer cottage flowers: golden rod, Michaelmas daisies, sunflowers and Japanese anemones, mallow and hollyhocks.

A back garden, painted by Myles Birket Foster. A woman works among the vegetables while her washing hangs out to dry. Besides cabbages, the vegetables most often grown were potatoes, beans, onions, carrots and parsnips, with perhaps some grain for the pig.

A native English plant, the pansy (centre), *bred to greater size and richer colours during the Victorian period; the sunflower* (bottom left), *which, with the hollyhock, was one of the most conspicuous and showy of cottage garden flowers; the cornflower* (below), *one of the many wild flowers that cottagers established in their gardens.*

the cottage garden was to become a symbol of the rustic delights of the countryside as portrayed in the paintings in watercolour of, among others, Myles Birket Foster.

> Bring orchids, bring the foxglove spire,
> The little speedwell's darling blue,
> Deep tulips dash'd with fiery dew
> Laburnums, dropping-wells of fire

wrote Tennyson, lauding the cottage gardens of the south.

Miss Mitford described a garden in her village 'full of common flowers, tulips, pinks, larkspurs, peonies, stocks and carnations with an arbour of privet, not unlike a sentry box, where one lives in a delicious green light, and looks out on the gayest of all gay flower-beds'. And the cottage walls were covered with hollyhocks, roses, honeysuckles and an apricot tree. Polyanthus, auricula, hyacinth, and ranunculus were popular, too. Twenty years later, the number of flowers cultivated by cottage gardeners had much increased, and included the dahlia and the pansy, which were both much admired.

With the influential writings of William Robinson and the writings and garden designs of Gertrude Jekyll at the end of the nineteenth century, the abundance and the abandon of the cottage garden were to be directly imported into the planting schemes of much larger and grander gardens.

Apart from bringing joy to the cottage owner and to passers-by, the cottage garden was one of the most important resources a labouring family had. They seldom bought vegetables, but usually

The Christmas or Lenten rose (top right), *one of the first plants to flower after the cold winter; a favourite since medieval times, the marigold* (bottom right) *was also used for cooking; the scarlet poppy* (below), *which would also have bordered the cornfields in summer.*

grew all their own: potatoes, cabbages, onions, leeks and parsnips, which were made into nourishing potages. Beans were almost as popular as potatoes, and in the nineteenth century the cottagers began to grow tomatoes from plants that they bought.

As with the vegetables, so with the fruit trees: they liked to have a few of every kind. Plums were favourites because the fruit sold well in the market, while gooseberries, redcurrants and raspberries, which especially appealed to the tastes of children, were made into jam. There was generally some rhubarb in every cottage garden; for centuries it had been grown for medicinal purposes and now it began to be used in cooking. Wild strawberries were found in the countryside and replanted at home. Flora Thompson wrote of the herb patch in the cottage garden, 'stocked with thyme and parsley and sage for cooking, rosemary to flavour the home-made lard, lavender to scent the best clothes and peppermint, pennyroyal, horehound, camomile, tansy, balm and rue for physic'. Lavender, tansy and meadowsweet were strewn on the floor to keep away pests.

In many villages, the process of enclosure of fields and commons had robbed the poor cottager of small parcels of land or common grazing rights, and a feature of Victorian village life was the frequent attempt to provide allotments. Farmers sometimes fought against them as it was reckoned they would distract labourers from their work; but in other quarters the provision of food was linked with moral reformation, for gardening kept men away from the alehouse. An eighth of an acre (twenty rods) was the ideal size to provide for a family of five; or so thought J. C. Loudon, who was one of those who crusaded for land for the cottagers. This would enable them to keep a pig and some poultry as well as grow potatoes and other vegetables.

However, Thomas Hardy's Tess found that during her absence her family had 'eaten all the seed potatoes – that last lapse of the improvident'. So Tess herself worked on an allotment, among thirty or forty other villagers, to grow food for them. Digging usually began at six o'clock when the day's work had been done, and extended into the dusk or moonlight. Since most farmers would not allow the men to borrow their horses to break up the soil, hand-digging was necessary. Some resorted to other devices for ploughing, and there was once seen in Suffolk the quaint sight of an old and quiet sow trained to walk on the land while a donkey walked in the furrow. In Tysoe, south Warwickshire, during the later decades of the last century, if a man tilled an acre with his own hands, his wife baked bread from the corn he raised, and he fed his pig with the inferior vegetables, then he might make a profit of two shillings and ninepence per week.

Commentators such as Richard Jefferies were confident that benevolence and inducements would help to improve the well-being of the cottager: 'Perhaps one of the best means devised has been that of cottage flower shows. These are, of course, not confined to flowers; in fact, the principal part of such shows consists of table vegetables and fruit. By rigidly excluding all gardeners, and all persons not strictly cottage people, the very best results have often been arrived at in this way. For if there is one thing in which the labourer takes an interest it is his garden and allotment. To offer him prizes for the finest productions of his garden touches the most sensitive part of his moral organization.' Working families might then be better able to fend for themselves.

By the mid-nineteenth century, village horticultural societies had begun to give prizes for gooseberries, cabbages and leeks as well as flowers. Francis Kilvert went to the flower show in Hay-on-Wye in 1870 and saw 'a nice large tent, the poles prettily wreathed with hop vine and the flowers, fruit and vegetables prettily arranged'. Flower shows had long been a part of rural life, although in earlier times interest had been confined to the so-called 'florist's flowers': the hyacinth, tulip, ranunculus, anemone, auricula, carnation, pink and polyanthus. The florists –

'Triumph', one of a series of watercolours painted by Miss E. D. Herschel of events in the Oxfordshire village of Littlemore in the 1880s. The little girl in the sun bonnet is Florence Wilson, who is holding the pot of balsam that won her first prize at the flower show.

George Vicat Cole's painting 'The Cottage Well'. Beside the well, conveniently situated in the cottager's garden, is a pail, a tin mug and a flagon. The rhubarb on the edge of the path would have been grown for medicinal purposes. In the vegetable plot are a hoe and dibber for planting out seedlings.

cottagers, weavers, lace-makers – had a tradition of carefully nurturing and developing these species. During the nineteenth century the cottage gardeners extended their skills to the cultivation of other flowers, and the pansy, chrysanthemum, dahlia, fuchsia, sweet william, iris, hollyhock, phlox and pelargonium were prized equally.

William Howitt points to plants bearing the names of the Derbyshire villagers who bred them: Hifton, Barker and Redgate for carnations, polyanthus and ranunculus. It is in cottage gardens that species are often rediscovered. A Mrs Ewing, who founded a society in the late nineteenth century to search out species of flowers on the point of disappearing, wrote that it was cottage gardens which 'have kept for us the Blue Primroses, the highly fragrant summer roses (including Rose de Meaux and the red and copper Brier), countless beautiful varieties of sweet, various and hardy flowers which are now returning. . . from the village to the hall. It is still in cottage gardens chiefly that the Crown Imperial hangs its royal head.' Howitt noted that in cottage windows two or three geraniums in pots were often to be seen. Pot plants were also kept in porches, where they could be admired by those who passed by in the village street.

Myles Birket Foster's engraving, 'At the Cottage Door', illustrates the thatched beehives, which William Cobbett stated should be made of 'clean unblighted rye-straw' to be replaced every three or four months.

In some cottage gardens, the owners kept bees, in woven straw skeps or neatly thatched hives, which provided sugar in the form of honey and pollinated the fruit trees. Some flowers and herbs were grown specially for their pollen; borage, golden rod, thyme, wallflowers, mignonettes and clover. William Howitt wrote of a typical keeper of bees: 'He has stored his little sheltered garden with all sorts of flowers that bees love, or that come out early in the year for them. On the sunny side of his little domain you see his rustic shed with its row of hives; all neatly thatched, and all sending out their busy stream of honey-gatherers.'

Most hives were destroyed when winter came, a practice at complete variance with what bee-keepers do today, so each year a bee-keeper needed to replenish the hives with a new swarm. In *Far from the Madding Crowd*, Hardy described the scene: 'The

Weatherbury bees were late in their swarming this year. It was in the latter part of June... that Bathsheba was standing in her garden, watching a swarm in the air and guessing their probable settling place. Not only were they late this year, but unruly... Bathsheba resolved to hive the bees herself, if possible. She had dressed the hives with herbs and honey, fetched a ladder, brush, and crook, made herself impregnable with armour of leather gloves, straw hat, and large gauze veil – once green but now faded to snuff colour – and ascended a dozen rungs of the ladder.' The earlier in the year, the better the chance of a good return in honey and wax from the bees who could be tempted into a new hive. As they said in country areas:

> A swarm in May is worth a load of hay.
> A swarm in June is worth a silver spoon.
> A swarm in July isn't worth a fly.

A caged bird beside the door was also a common feature of the cottage garden: sometimes a songbird, but often a thrush or a jay. The cottage birds' cages might be fancy or plain but were rarely large, so a bird would lead a very restricted existence. They were the poor relations of the songbirds in gilded cages that still decorated the drawing-rooms of the well-to-do. Some birds, like the robin and the jay, also still had magical significance according to folklore, while sparrows and blackbirds might occasionally make a tasty meal in difficult times. That was the essence of the cottage garden: beauty and necessity were brought together there.

The beehives were placed on a bench to prevent rats and mice from robbing the hives of honey. Towards the end of the century wooden hives, devised for more scientific bee-keeping, were brought into common use.

WOMENFOLK

T HE WOMEN OF THE VILLAGE had lives of seemingly unending hard work, mainly of a domestic nature. A husband's 'toil is for the most part over when he leaves the fields,' wrote Richard Jefferies, 'but the woman's is never finished'. As the woman moved around her cottage, washing and cleaning, making up the fire and standing over the hot range, the baby of the family would be crying for attention. The girls helped their mothers and were hardly more than infants themselves when they were expected to take care of other infants: 'The little creatures go lugging about great fat babies that really seem as heavy as themselves. You may see them on the commons, or little open green spots in the lanes near their homes, congregating together, two or three juvenile nurses, with their charges, carrying them along, or letting them roll in the sward.' The 'little creatures' were 'too old to need nursing, and too young to begin nursing others,' wrote William Howitt.

Women with their small children would gather at the village pump or well and talk, before walking home with their shoulders weighed down by the heavy buckets. Gossiping provided a brief respite from everyday chores. Thomas Hardy commented on the posture and gait of the women, 'their knuckles being mostly on their hips (an attitude which gave them the aspect of two-handled mugs), and their shoulders against doorposts' as they relayed the news of the village to their neighbours.

Keeping the family fed took up much of the day, but there was little variety in what the labourer's wife had to cook and the food was often meagre. A medical enquiry in 1863 revealed that on average each adult in a labouring family ate over twelve pounds of bread a week, and another six pounds of potatoes, which came from the garden or were grown in an allotment. Meat consumption averaged only twelve ounces a week. The poor were advised, in a recipe written by 'A Lady', to put a crust of bread into a pot where salt-beef was boiling to attract some of the fat. When swelled out, she remarked, it 'will be no unpalatable dish to those who rarely taste meat'. The slowness of country people was ascribed by some to their limited and repetitive diet.

Straw-plaiters, painted by Carlton A. Smith. Straw-plaiting was one of the village crafts in which the wives of tradesmen and labourers were engaged until the end of the century. Bedfordshire was the centre of the industry, and the plait was mainly used in hatmaking.

Carlton A. Smith '91.

By the late nineteenth century, there seems to have been some improvement in cottage families' eating habits. More meat was being eaten and the consumption of dairy produce had risen; items such as jam, coffee, cocoa and margarine had been introduced. Tea-kettle broth, made from bread, hot water, salt and – if you were lucky – milk, was becoming a country memory. Jefferies' description of cottage food in the 1880s was probably only a slightly rosy version of the truth: '... the fare will often be found of a substantial character. There may be a piece of mutton – not, of course, the prime cut, but wholesome meat – cabbages, parsnips, carrots (labourers like a profusion of vegetables), all laid out in a decent manner. The food is plain, but solid and plentiful... [Yet] the cooking in the best cottages would not commend itself to the student of that art.' He recognized that there would be differences between one household and another and that 'in those where the woman is shiftless, it would be deemed simply intolerable' by the author and others of his kind.

In the early part of the century, it was common for women to work in the fields, especially in the northern counties. Arthur Munby, who interviewed a number of working women during a trip north in 1862, wrote: 'In one of the large ploughed fields there, I saw a woman all alone, diligently plying her hoe... I met her in the lane soon after, coming home, for it was dusk. A nice looking young married woman she was, with light hair and sunburnt face; wearing a crumpled bonnet, a tattered cotton frock, and strong earthy boots; carrying her hoe, and a knife in her hand

for cutting weeds. She had been working there by herself all day, since eight in the morning, except dinnertime: stubbing wickwood and hoeing. Put her children out to nurse meanwhile. Had worked afield all her life, woman and wench: hoeing, digging taters, harvesting.' Nevertheless, by this date it was becoming unusual to find women regularly employed in agriculture. The increasing use of machinery, and the pressure to keep men's wages up, excluded women – and certainly married women – from most kinds of agricultural work. There was also a growing emphasis on the value of domesticity, the Victorian gospel of respectability actively encouraged by the middle classes, and a belief that wives and mothers had a noble and essential occupation in the home, caring for husband and children.

The need to supplement the family income was often acute, however, and there were many ways that this could be done other than in agricultural work. In wooded areas, for instance, they peeled bark from trees to supplement the family income. Marty South, the heroine of Hardy's *The Woodlanders*, 'turned her hand to anything' in the woodland trades: she peeled bark, planted trees, and chopped and split hazel branches for thatching spars. Where willow grew, women and children peeled and harvested the osiers to make baskets. In fishing villages, women and children wound twine, and the women braided nets.

Throughout the early years of the nineteenth century, women continued to help on the land during the busy seasons, especially during the harvest. In the hop fields, in Kent, Worcestershire and

Village women ranged below in their most frequent guises: carrying and leading children, fetching water, taking produce to market or bringing back their gleanings from the harvest field. Time was too precious ever to go anywhere empty-handed. Drawings by E. Chambers.

Herefordshire, women's work included not only tying and harvesting hops but also shaving the hop poles, and mending all the sacks and bin cloths.

Among the cottage industries that occupied village women, spinning and weaving survived in many places until the end of the Victorian period, though mainly for the family's needs. The factories had taken away most of the home-based textile working. In northern parts of England, the traditional craft of quilting was a particular cause for pride.

It was in the Dales that William Howitt came upon some curious practices associated with knitting. In that region the women knitted incessantly, and there were knitting schools where the children were taught and where knitting songs were sung in chorus. After the children had been put to bed, the women assembled in one of the cottages: 'They sit rocking to and fro like so many weird wizards. They burn no candle, but knit by the light of the peat fire. And this rocking motion is connected with a mode of knitting peculiar to the place, called swaving, which is difficult to describe. Ordinary knitting is performed by a variety of little motions, but this is a single uniform tossing motion of both the hands at once, and the body often accompanying it with a sort of sympathetic action... They knit with crooked pins called pricks; and use a knitting-sheath of a dagger, curved to the side, and fixed in a belt called the cowband.' In this manner they knitted stockings, jackets, nightcaps and a kind of cap 'worn by the negroes, called bump-caps', for the Kendal market.

In rural areas near large towns, especially in the later years of the Victorian period, many women did 'slop work': the making of garments from offcuts and old pieces of material. Plaiting straw was another female occupation, common in Bedfordshire, Buckinghamshire, Hertfordshire and Essex. An elderly Hertfordshire woman, at the end of Queen Victoria's reign, had spent all her life plaiting straw and recalled that it was used mainly in the hat industry. Her first lesson had been at the age of three, when she was 'given three or four splints of straw and was taught how to twist them under and over... to the words and tune of a little song, "under one and over two, pull it tight and that will do".' Before 1870, and compulsory schooling under the Education Act of that year, children in those parts of the country would go to plaiting

A young woman knits stockings at the door of her cottage in a painting by Henry Bright. Knitting was particularly associated with the north of England and the Dales, where the men, women and children all knitted: wagoners had once knitted as they went along with their teams.

G. W. Mote's painting of women sitting outside their cottages making gloves, sewing the leather and stretching the fingers over a frame. Fine handwork was often done out of doors, if not at the window, for the sake of the light. Glovemaking was especially common in Oxfordshire and Wiltshire as a means of adding to the husband's wages. Sometimes the women earned more than the men.

The lace-maker working at her cottage door; traditionally this was a craft for women, particularly in Devon, Northamptonshire, Oxfordshire, Bedfordshire and Buckinghamshire. In order to learn the intricate skill of making delicate pillow lace, girls as young as five or six would begin to learn the craft.

schools, crowded and often exploitative establishments run by a 'dame', where, as they learnt the skills of plaiting, they occasionally acquired the rudiments of reading.

Lace-making was taught to girls in the same way, and they went on to spend a lifetime working with their fine thread and bobbins. Bobbin lace, or pillow lace, as described by one late Victorian collector of handicrafts, 'is made on a round cushion of about twelve inches to twenty-four inches in diameter. This cushion is called a pillow, hence the term "pillow" lace. On the pillow are a large number of pins, these being used to form the pattern of the lace required to be made. The threads are twisted around the pins, and across one another in a dexterous manner. One end of each thread is fastened to the pillow, the other being wound round the top of a bobbin.'

Hand-made lace, as opposed to the machine variety principally made in Nottingham, adorned many a Victorian lady's costume. Its fineness and quality were testimony to the skilled, slow work involved. For pieces of lace each as wide as a fingernail, a lace-maker said: 'It takes between sixty and seventy stitches to make six head-pins' forming the pattern, 'and it takes me twelve hours a working very hard indeed to make a yard of it.' For this she earned fourpence a yard. The women's and children's lace-making, and straw plait work too, could bring in as much income to the family as an able-bodied labouring man on eleven or twelve shillings a week.

Jefferies tells a story of a woman who 'kept her cottage entirely by her own exertions; her husband doing nothing but drink. He took her money from her by force, nor could she hide it anywhere but what he would hunt it out. At last in despair she dropped the silver in the jug on the wash-hand basin, and had the satisfaction of seeing him turn everything topsy-turvy in a vain attempt to find it. As he never washed, it never occurred to him to look in the water-jug.' Drink was something that many women contended with.

The women would occasionally take up a song as they worked. A traditional ditty sung by lace-makers in the Buckinghamshire village of Weston Underwood ran:

A lad down at Olney looked over a wall,
And saw nineteen little golden girls playing at ball.
Golden girls, golden girls, will you be mine?
You shall neither wash dishes nor wait on the swine.
But sit on a cushion and sew a fine seam,
Eat white bread and butter and strawberries and cream.

In Dorset villages, women and children made buttons; in parts of Oxfordshire and Somerset, particularly around Yeovil, they made leather gloves, the best
ones of kid. But in the later years of the Victorian age,
many of these cottage industries were in decline, the
victims of factory machinery and the vagaries of
fashion. The invention of Ashton's button-making
machine in 1851 was the death-knell of the Dorset
button industry, which caused extensive misery in
many villages. And in Buckinghamshire, where there
were over 10,000 lacemakers in 1851, the number had
halved by 1881, and by 1901 only 789 were left. The
collapse was even more spectacular in straw-plaiting:
from the industry's height in 1871, when there were
more than 20,000 women employed in Bedfordshire, numbers
were reduced to only 485 plaiters in 1901.

A woman spinning, engraved for the Book of English Trades *published in 1839. The women often worked directly for the woolcomber, who would supply them with the wool to spin into skeins. This in turn might go to the winder, who would prepare it for the weaver. The author suggested that women with expertise could earn a shilling a day, while children who were taught young would soon earn from sixpence to one and sixpence a week.*

The hard-working cottage woman with a few pence to spare
was, in Jefferies' story, the despair of shop-keepers. She would go
into a shop and examine half-a-dozen dress fabrics, rubbing each
between her work-hardened fingers and thumb till the shopkeeper
winced, expecting to see it torn. After trying several and getting
the counter covered she would push them aside, contemptuously
remarking, "I don't like this yer shallygallee (flimsy) stuff. Haven't
'ee got any gingham tackle?" Whereat the poor draper would cast
down a fresh roll of stoutest material with the reply: "Here,
ma'am. Here's something that will wear like pinwire".

Many of the country women valued the cottage crafts, not only
for the money that was brought into the home, but also for the
enjoyment of working together in one of the cottages. It afforded
them the companionship enjoyed by menfolk in their work, but
which was denied to women doing nothing but domestic chores in
their own homes.

CHILDREN

VILLAGE CHILDREN HAD LITTLE more than their surroundings and their imaginings with which to content themselves. Francis Kilvert came across this happy scene one day in January 1870: 'In the Common Field in front of the cottages I found two little figures in the dusk. One tiny urchin was carefully binding a handkerchief round the face of an urchin even more tiny than himself. It was Fred and Jerry Savine. "What are you doing to him?", I asked Fred. "Please, Sir," said the child solemnly. "Please, Sir, we'm gwine to play at blind man's buff." The two children were quite alone. The strip of dusky meadow was like a marsh and every footstep trod the water out of the soaked land, but the two little images went solemnly on with their game as if they were in a magnificent playground with a hundred children to play with. Oh, the wealth of a child's imagination and capacity for enjoyment of trifles.'

Sometimes their fun served all the family – blackberrying, nutting or picking sloes and crab apples in autumn – though often it was to gather for themselves a little of what the countryside had to offer. Sybil Marshall and her friends in the Cambridgeshire fenlands explored and enjoyed the world that lay all around them. Looking back to her childhood she wrote: 'We dug up tansy roots to eat, and filled our pockets with buckwheat whenever we could. We sucked the taste of honey from the tip ends of the white dead-nettle flowers, and suffered agonies peeling thistle buds down to get at the little white nut in the middle. Then off to gather different sorts of flowers again to dress ourselves up to play "Kings and Queens".'

Occasionally, the cottage children would have pennies to spend. Miss Mitford was very much amused by how very poor children became acquainted with the rate of exchange between the smaller denomination of coin and commodities such as cakes, nuts and gingerbread they bought at the village shop. 'No better judge of the currency question than a country brat of three years old,' she wrote; and she seemed almost to admire the anger of a child who detected that he or she had been cheated by a shopkeeper amusing himself at the child's expense.

Country boys with their rabbits, a painting by E. C. Barnes. William Cobbett wrote, 'of all animals rabbits are those that boys are most fond of. The produce has not long to be waited for . . . and they really cost nothing; for, as to the oats, where is the boy that cannot, in harvest time, pick up enough along the lanes to serve his rabbits for a year?'

Children played in the Victorian countryside – and shopkeeping was one of their games. They also worked. Labouring families were among the largest in the country for the reason that almost as soon as they could walk and talk the children would be expected to help in some way. The help might be in the form of small domestic chores, though in areas of cottage industry girls would be made to learn handicraft skills from infancy. And there were always jobs to be done outside – gathering faggots or running errands – and pennies to be earned from tasks such as scaring birds or picking stones from the fields. Farmers would prevent children working together, since they would soon turn to play: 'Two boys is half a boy, and three boys no boy at all.' At haymaking and harvest, everyone, of any age, took part in the communal effort.

In the large arable farming areas of the eastern counties, especially Norfolk and Lincolnshire, children were involved in gang work in the 1840s to the 1860s. Large groups of them, and women as well, were recruited for back-breaking farm tasks: potato-setting, turnip-cutting, weeding, stone-picking. Public opinion was galvanized when it became known that children were being forced to walk miles to and from work for slave wages, and witnesses saw 'the big ones come dragging the little ones home, and sometimes taking them on their backs when they are overtired'. In 1867 public agitation resulted in the first legislation restricting children's work in agriculture. The 1833 Factory Act had already abolished child labour in factories.

The process of reform was continued in the education legislation, of which the 1870 Education Act was the cornerstone: there was to be provision for every child, and compulsory school attendance until at least the age of ten. Some villages had schools of ancient foundation or parish schools supported from the rates or charity, others had a school endowed and maintained by a local landowner or patron. A growing number of country parishes had 'National' schools, which were kept going by collections and contributions to augment the funds made available by the government.

A sketch by James Ward of a young countryman in the early part of the nineteenth century (left). Dressed in a waistcoat and long coat, he is clearly wearing his best clothes.

A study of a country boy on a horse by Robert Hills (below). He wears a smock, the traditional clothing for farmers, labourers and children, which had largely disappeared by the end of the Victorian age.

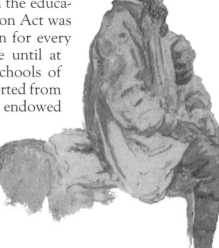

Apart from a reluctance on the part of some of the children to be confined to school, it was hard for parents not to keep them at home, to clean the house or look after the baby, or send them out to work – at first one or two days a week, then three or four – until they were old enough to go all the time. In winter there were a few for whom no boots could be found.

A typical village elementary school in the nineteenth century consisted of one classroom in which all the children, ranging in age from five to thirteen years, were in the charge of a single teacher, sometimes assisted by one or two young monitors. Larger establishments had separate classrooms – and separate entrances – for boys and girls, though the ages were still mixed.

Every classroom would have a portrait of Queen Victoria, and a map on the wall showed that a large part of the world owed allegiance to her. Pupils were provided with slates and chalks, and there would be counting frames for the youngest mathematicians.

In lessons, the emphasis was almost entirely on the three Rs, which were regarded as quite separate skills and had to be learnt in sequence. It was common for children from the country to leave

Girls returning to a cottage bearing corn gleaned from the harvest fields. In the words of Tom Taylor, 'Their talk ran on their harvest spoil, | The bushes gleaned and shelled; | Each boasting how her childish toil | The household store had swelled.'

school able to read, but barely able to sign their names. Clergymen and, later, inspectors oversaw the running of the schools. They usually encouraged learning by rote – tables, capital cities, the kings and queens of England – and the cane for young offenders.

Charles Dickens recaptured in *The Old Curiosity Shop* a summer's day at school: 'Then began the hum of conning over lessons and getting them by heart, the whispered jest and stealthy game, and all the noise and drawl of school; and in the midst of the din sat the poor school master, the very image of meekness... Oh! how some of these idle fellows longed to be outside, and how they looked at the open door and window, as if they half meditated rushing violently out, plunging into the woods, and being wild boys and savages from that time forth.'

By 1861, more than half the schools in England were run by women. At these 'dame' schools, the girls learnt to sew and knit, and had some religious instruction, but often little else was offered in the way of education. Mostly, the emphasis was on preparing them for a life of self-sacrifice and domesticity. A rhyme from a reading book published in 1871 ran:

Elder sisters, you may work,
Work and help your mothers,
Darn the stockings, mend the shirts,
father's things, and brother's

In general, more attention was undoubtedly given to boys than to girls. Miss Mitford, for one, pleaded 'guilty to a strong partiality towards that unpopular class of beings, country boys: I have a large acquaintance amongst them, and I can almost say, that I know good of many and harm of none... They are patient, too, and bear their fate as scape-goats (for all sins whatsoever are laid as matters of course to their door), whether at home or abroad, with amazing resignation...'

The preference went further than this. At dinner time, father would be given his food first, then the sons; the daughters and mother dutifully brought up the rear, eating whatever might be

Children drawing water from a well, a watercolour by Myles Birket Foster. Fetching water was essentially the province of women and, with them, children. Before piped water, it was not unusual to walk a quarter of a mile or more for water from a well, spring or stream.

All but the very smallest children would be put to carrying out chores such as collecting firewood. Furze, fir cones, even straw and animal dung were brought into the cottages for burning on the fire. The watercolour, dated 1863, is by John Henry Mole.

left for them. Richard Jefferies, writing in *The Toilers of the Field*, reported that: 'If a thoughtful English peasant woman rejoiced that in her house a son was born, it would be, not because "she had gotten a man from the Lord", but a thanksgiving that it was not a girl.' Flora Thompson, writing about Juniper Hill, Oxfordshire, recalled: 'If there was any inconvenience it must not fall on the boys; if there was a limited quantity of anything, the boys must still have their full share.' Parents were loath to let the boys leave home because they contributed to the family income. 'The girls, while at home, could earn nothing' (for theirs was a village with no cottage industry employing women and girls), and therefore work opportunities were found outside the home. The mother would say to her daughter, as soon as she was old enough, 'About time you was earnin' your own livin', me gel', or, to a neighbour, 'I shan't be sorry when our young so-and-so gets her knees under somebody else's table. Five slices for breakfast this morning if you please'.

Design for a village school, by the architect P. F. Robinson, published in 1830. The projecting roof formed 'a dry walk for the children in inclement weather'.

Going into service was always an important form of employment for girls, at first locally and then further afield. Hannah Cullwick, a Victorian maid-of-all-work who lived most of her life in London, had started as a servant when she was eight, in 1841, in her home parish of Shifnal, Shropshire. At fourteen she got her first proper place away in service as a nursery-maid in a local big house, and, after a number of engagements, at seventeen she accompanied her new mistress to London. Thereafter, she only ever revisited Shropshire occasionally, until she eventually retired there in old age.

Work started at an early age, and Hannah's story, as told in the diaries she left, was typical of the time. It was usual to start in service at a house nearby, visiting home and younger brothers and sisters whenever the opportunity was given, and leaving behind a few pence saved from the wages. Boys might follow their fathers on to the land or into a craft trade, and many left the countryside behind. Childhood was quickly over in Victorian England.

Reading primers such as the one from which this page is taken were used in most schools. Reading Made most Easy went through nearly a hundred editions in the first four decades of the nineteenth century.

13

Reading Made most Easy.

EASY LESSONS,
Consisting of Words not exceeding
TWO LETTERS;
Being the most proper for Children who have just learned the Alphabet.

I.
As we do, so do ye.
Be to us as we to ye.
C is as we go by.
Do ye go to it, or no.

II.
Go ye as we go to it.
He is to be as I am.
I am to do as ye do.
K is to be at it.

a

A scene in a boys' school-room with boisterous pupils on benches at a central desk and the schoolmaster beyond. A watercolour by G. G. Kilburne painted in the mid-nineteenth century.

CHAPTER 3
THE FARM

FARM AND FARMYARD

THE FARM THAT Bathsheba Everdene took over in Thomas Hardy's *Far from the Madding Crowd* was almost exactly the 'typical' farm for Dorset selected by an 1868 Royal Commission to illustrate farm employment. It extended over 660 acres, of which 500 were arable, and the farmer employed twenty-nine men and boys full-time as well as fifteen extra – eleven of them women – in harvest time. His annual wages bill was £788. Human muscle and horse muscle supplied the power for farm work; steam had yet to arrive, and very little of the work was aided by machinery. On modern farms, machinery has replaced men and horses, and such a farm today would have little or no full-time paid help. No twentieth-century farmer would contemplate the size of the labour force – or the corresponding wage bill – that Bathsheba Everdene's Weatherbury, or this similar establishment chosen by the Royal Commissioners, had had.

Farmers were in their heyday in the middle years of Queen Victoria's reign. Home demand for their produce, and especially for grain, was buoyant, while they had few foreign competitors for supplying the national food market. Many of the substantial farmers were wealthy men, and their landlords enjoyed healthy rent rolls. In Victorian England, the age of the great landed estates, a farmer was more likely to be a tenant than the owner of his farm. Farmer and landlord would work together to improve the land, and their profits.

Status and profitability still meant that good farmers would have to work hard. William Howitt reported a particularly assiduous Cambridgeshire farmer's daily routine: 'Rose at three o'clock. . . roused the girls to milking, roused the horsekeeper, fed the horses while he was getting up; called the boy to suckle the calves and clean out the cow-house; lighted the pipe, walked

The farmer brings the heavy horses back to the yard after a day's work in the fields, an oil painting by Edwin Meadows dated 1885. The horse provided the power for most farm tasks. At the end of the century there were still around a million horses working on farms.

round the garden to see what was wanted there; went up to the paddock to see if the weaning calves were well; went down to the ferry to see if the boy had scooped and cleaned the boat; returned to the farm, examined the shoulders, heels, traces, chaff and corn of eight horses going to plough, mended the acre-staff, cut some thongs, whipcorded the ploughboys' whips, pumped the troughs full, saw the hogs fed, examined the swill tubs, and then the cellar; ordered a quarter of malt, for the hogs want grains, and the men want beer; filled the pipe again, returned to the river and bought a lighter of turf for dairy fires, and another of sedge for ovens; hunted out the wheelbarrows, and set them a trundling; returned to the farm, called the men to breakfast, and cut the boys' bread and cheese, and saw the wooden bottles filled; sent one plough to the three roods, another to the three half-acres, and so on; shut the gates, and the clock struck five.' That was the hour for breakfast, after which the day's real work would begin.

The Victorians knew how much depended on their efforts, and what temptations and pitfalls there were to taking life easy and spending the profits of farming on non-essentials:

> Boy to the barn,
> Girl to the yarn,
> And your rent will be netted.
> Boy, tally-ho,
> Miss, piano,
> And you'll all be gazetted.

(Above and right) Pages from a sketchbook by Robert Hills of farmyards in the first half of the nineteenth century. Hills was an artist who specialized in depictions of farmyards with all their rich variety of buildings and activities.

Pen and ink drawing by Edward Duncan of a barn being thatched (below). It was crucial to keep any storage building water-tight, and thatching would have to be replaced every twenty to thirty years.

Two from the hundreds of different configurations of carts and wagons; the variations were often regional. The Norfolk and Suffolk wagon (below left) is described in J. F. Burke's British Husbandry *of 1834 as being designed for countryside where 'the roads are good and the country very level': This wagon had the capacity of ten quarters of wheat with four horses drawing it on a turnpike and five on by-roads. The two-wheeled cart (below centre) had to be pulled by two horses. An early machine for turning hay after scything (below right) while it lay in the fields.*

Whatever the small luxuries farmers permitted themselves and their families, their houses and farmsteads tended to belong to a basic pattern. The larger and grander ones were virtually indistinguishable from the manor houses and great houses of the gentry. The standard layout of a lesser kind was described by Richard Jefferies: 'They consist as it were of two distinct houses under one roof. The front is the dwelling-house proper, usually containing a kitchen, sitting room and parlour. The back contains the wood-house (coal-house now), the brewhouse – where the beer was brewed – which frequently also had an oven, and, most important of all, the dairy. All this part of the place is paved in stone flags, and the dairy is usually furnished with lattice-work in front of the windows, so that they can be left open to admit the cool air and not thieves. Coolness is the great requisite in a dairy... In front of the dairy and brewhouse is a paved court... [where] the buckets are washed and other similar duties performed. The labourers come here to receive their daily allowance of beer.' Below them in the scale of farmhouses, Jefferies identified those 'low thatched buildings, little better than large cottages, and indeed frequently converted into dwellings for labourers. These are generally found on small farms, and in districts where there are a number of small landed proprietors.'

Among the finest legacies of the Victorian age are the farmhouses that were rebuilt at that time, sometimes, following enclosure, to bring them conveniently close to the farmer's holding of land. They were reconstructed with more rooms and in a more deliberate, less haphazard, architectural style, both to correspond with the higher local standing and income of the farmer, and to meet changing ideas of respectability. Servants,

who had once shared the table and sleeping accommodation of the family, were frequently given separate quarters. Francis Kilvert was amused to visit Farmer Wall in his brand new Welsh border farmhouse: 'The father and children took me all over the new house. Lucretia showed me her bed, a French bed, blue and gold, the prettiest piece of furniture I saw. Wall pointed out to me with satisfaction the door with a lock which separated the sleeping rooms of the servant boys and girls.'

The principal change was, perhaps, that Victorian farmers were almost exclusively men. Bathsheba Everdene would not have been unusual in an earlier century, but as a woman farmer, and thus an employer, she was certainly remarkable in the mid-Victorian world described by Hardy in his novels. Apart from being male, there was no characteristic shared by all farmers. Some were rosy-cheeked Farmer Georges, others keen appliers of the latest in scientific technology. Many knew only the ways of their fore-fathers, a few read the agricultural journals and rushed to intro-duce the innovations that they recommended. The bigger the establishment, usually the more advanced the farming techniques.

At the heart of every farm was the farmyard. The types of build-ings, and the names given to them, varied from one region to another, but the concept of an organized yard was almost univer-sal. The barn, with its great double doors to allow vehicles access and the draught to blow through for threshing, was a common feature. Rough, open-sided stalls might be all that was provided for the cattle, for milking was often done in the fields. Stables, tack rooms, hay lofts, dairies, cheese rooms, pigstys, were part of the general pattern. The yard itself might have great piles of manure in it, with the dung-hill cock crowing on top. This was much as farmyards had ever been.

From 1840 the application of rational and scientific theories to farmyards and buildings, as well as to farming techniques them-selves, was an increasing preoccupation. Enterprising farmers and, more particularly, interested landowners, began to promote agricultural improvement, which included investing in model farms. All over the country are to be seen the permanent, stone or brick – and occasionally even concrete – structures that they put up, ranged around interlocking yards and providing good shelter for beasts and produce. In the most advanced, and often least

A farmhouse interior, painted by Edmund Swift. Grace is said before the midday meal, while the farm servants take their ale in another part of the room. Although the table is covered with a white cloth and set with china, the room is essentially workaday, with hams hung from the beams and guns in their traditional place on a rack over the fireplace.

profitable ventures, farmers attempted to combine all the farming functions under one roof, to make a fully interactive system where even the dung from the stalled cattle might be pumped out on to the nearby fields. Sometimes these ventures were undertaken as much for show and as interesting experiments – toys for the amusement of landowners – as in the hope of proper returns on their investment. Nevertheless, the profits generated by farming were often returned to the land, in the form of investment in farm buildings and houses as well as in machines and fertilizers.

The high point of Victorian farming was in the era of the aptly named 'high farming'. After much agitation, the protectionist Corn Laws were repealed in the 1840s – and, contrary to the fears

Further improvements in farming: a combined winnower, weighing and bagging machine made by T. Corbett of Shrewsbury and illustrated in the 1908 edition of Stephens' Book of the Farm. *Described as saving the work of two men, machines such as this contributed to the decline in the agricultural workforce.*

of the rural lobby, did not result in disaster for English farmers. Growing towns and industrial workforces needed to be fed, and the farmer at home could provide that food as cheaply as any competitor from abroad. Indeed, there were no serious foreign competitors to match the efficiency of English agriculture.

Victorian agriculture in the 1850s and 1860s, when high farming was practised, was characterized by high inputs and high returns. Farmers began using more and more fertilizers to increase the yield of their crops – phosphatic nodules and lime from the ground, imported guano from Peruvian bird colonies. They grew root crops, and especially turnips, to feed the sheep and cattle that grazed on the grasslands and produced dung to add to the fertilizer. What they wanted – what the market demanded – was grain. Labour was used liberally, in maintaining the farm as well as the crops and livestock to a high standard. Some, wealthier, farmers were beginning to use machinery seriously, starting with threshing machinery and moving on to machines for reaping and ploughing. It seemed as if farming could not stop expanding.

However, with the opening up of the American plains and the superior growing conditions there, improved transatlantic shipping, and the coincidence of successive bad summers in England, cheaper grain from the New World devastated home production. Farmers took land out of cultivation, cut back on investment in buildings, and began to use the workforce more efficiently by switching away from labour-intensive crops and bothering less about the weeds and the look of their fields. Only livestock and, especially, dairy farmers were less hard hit.

Landowners found that their profits were falling, tenants were in arrears, there was no surplus to reinvest. Machinery became a long-term cost-effective alternative to the profligate use of labour. The doldrums lasted until the Second World War – and the picturesque disorder of the farmyard which artists loved to reproduce, and poets such as Tom Taylor to describe, became more rather than less common in the latter years of Victoria's reign:

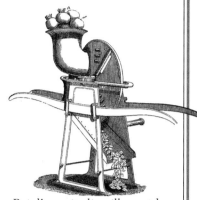

Baird's turnip-slicer illustrated in J. C. Loudon's Encyclopedia of Agriculture *of 1844. The cubed turnip would be used as animal fodder when the pasture failed at the end of summer. It was also recognized that a turnip crop added to the fertility of the soil. Loudon described turnips, along with clover, as 'one of the two main pillars of the best courses of British husbandry'.*

> I see the farmyard of my boyhood still,
> Its aspect facing to the sheep-fed hill;
> The thick leaf-piles that swayed with murmurous sound,
> Bee-haunted limes, elms where rooks wheeled and watched,
> Above the roofs, green-mossed and russet-thatched,
> That on grey posts the fold-yard shaded round:
> The open cart-shed – shed and gate in one;
> The pigs and heifers basking in the sun,
> Above the leg-deep litter, trod to paste:
> The ragged rails, the faggot-pile beyond;
> The hoof-poached edge of the green-mantled pond,
> Its marge and surface with white feathers dotted;
> The high-ridged barn with orange lichen spotted.

ANIMAL HUSBANDRY

O NE OF THE MOST VALUED and valuable of all animals in the Victorian village was the pig, important because it was a cottage as well as a farm animal. Pigs 'are great softeners of the temper and promoters of domestic harmony,' wrote William Cobbett in *Cottage Economy*. 'A couple of flitches of bacon are worth fifty thousand Methodist sermons and religious tracts.'

The beast might be left to forage for itself, though Cobbett's advice was that 'much must depend upon the situation of the cottage... Even in lanes, or on the sides of great roads, a pig will find a good part of his food from May to November; and, if he be yoked, the occupiers of the neighbourhood must be churlish and brutish indeed if they give the owner any annoyance.' More often, the pig was kept in a sty, within easy reach of all the kitchen scraps.

As an important member of a cottager's family, news of the pig's progress was eagerly sought by visitors. Often, tasty titbits were kept for it, as well as the usual waste and peelings, all in preparation for the day of slaughter. Flora Thompson wrote that the scene, 'with its mud and blood, flaring lights and dark shadows, was as savage as anything to be seen in an African jungle'. She was a child with a vivid imagination, and so, as the pig was slaughtered, scalded and butchered, she went to bed full of remorse for this animal that the whole family had become fond of. Yet she was grateful for the bacon, hams, sausages, lard and all the other parts that came from the pig – everything was used up except the squeak, it used to be said. The pig helped many country cottage families to get through the long winter months, with the warming fat content of the meat: 'The man who cannot live on solid fat bacon, well fed and well cured, wants the sweet sauce of labour, or is fit for the hospital.'

Cottagers might be in a position to keep a few other animals: a cow was a particular asset where they had rights to common grazing or could make an arrangement with a farmer. The cottage

Shepherds have gathered sheep into the fold on an autumn morning in a painting by John Linnell. The flock is feeding on what was left in the field at the end of the turnip harvest.

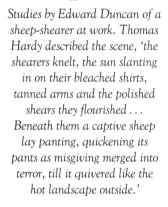

Studies by Edward Duncan of a sheep-shearer at work. Thomas Hardy described the scene, 'the shearers knelt, the sun slanting in on their bleached shirts, tanned arms and the polished shears they flourished . . . Beneath them a captive sheep lay panting, quickening its pants as misgiving merged into terror, till it quivered like the hot landscape outside.'

wives would frequently be able to keep hens or geese, which provided eggs and then meat when they were past laying. Most of the animals, though, were part of the stock in trade of farms.

Most Victorian farms were mixed, that is, crops were grown and animals kept. Depending on the type of land, and access to markets, the balance between crops and animals, and meat and other produce, would vary. Animals were integral to the high farming that dominated mid-Victorian agriculture, eating the clover and root crops such as turnips that were part of the sequence of crop rotation. They became even more important on later nineteenth-century farms as grain crops proved increasingly less profitable.

The killing of the pig. No part of the pig was wasted. Here the blood is being saved to make blood pudding. In addition there would be souse, griskins, blade-bones, spare-ribs, chines, belly-pieces, cheeks and most importantly the two sides, or flitches, for bacon.

Sheep were the animals most widely farmed. There were few areas of the country that could not support sheep, either for rearing, as was more common in the north and west of England, or for fattening, as in the east. While some breeds were prized for their wool, others were kept for meat. The shepherd was a lone man, who tended many hundreds of animals on the open grazing, often living out with them in his hut. One young Suffolk lad remembered: 'I was so young, that I dursn't stay out in the dark by myself. . . so for a little while my father used to come out with me at night, and sleep in the little ol' cabin along o' me. But I soon got used to it by myself, and I took no notice of the queer little noises you hear in the dark.'

Cattle were kept for beef, for their hides and for their milk. Until the latter years of the last century, liquid milk was only a paying proposition when farmers were within easy reach of a large town or a city (there were many urban dairies, as well, where cows were kept in filthy and cramped conditions). Butter and cheese were easier to keep and transport than milk, and therefore most farms had a dairy.

Cattle raised for meat and destined for London and the large urban markets were often bred in the upland regions of Wales, Scotland or in the north-west of England. They were then driven

The pig's hair was burnt or scalded off and the skin scraped clean. William Cobbett in Cottage Economy *preferred the burning method, peculiar, he said, to Hampshire, and the reason that bacon from that area was so excellent.*

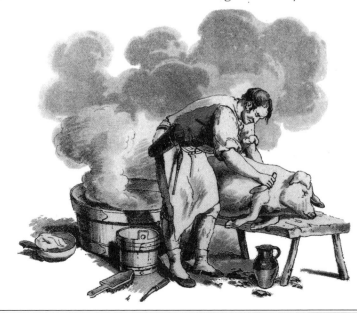

by the men and their working dogs south and east to be fattened on richer pastures before being taken to Smithfield or some other large market. Different parts of the country were thus tied together in an extended farming system that reached into the furthest corners of the land.

As part of the later Victorian shift towards more intensive livestock rearing, progressive farmers changed the look and layout of their farmyards. Gone were the all-purpose, cramped byres and cow-houses, and the open yards with shelter sheds around them that had been so common; instead tethered animals were cared for in covered sheds. The beasts were kept warmer, their feed could be controlled more easily, and the manure protected from what were proved to be the diluting effects of the rain and the sun. Scientific research into agriculture, which had started with grain-growing, was beginning to be directed towards animal management. Silage was being introduced to feed animals, and the first of the cake feeds were coming on to the market. By the last years of the nineteenth century, animal husbandry was beginning to approach today's standards.

At the same time, efforts to improve the breeding of farm animals continued. Prize animals, often of tremendous weight and size – and of a shape that looks distinctly odd to modern eyes –

A labourer admiring his pigs, painted by James Ward. In Cottage Economy, William Cobbett recommended that the pig should be bought in spring or late winter, 'being then four months old, he will be a year old before killing time'. If the animal can walk two hundred yards at a time, 'he is not well-fatted'.

Several Victorian artists made their living by capturing for a proud owner the conformation of his favourite livestock. Here, the herdsman is included in the composition together with the bull, the cow and the calf, all prize animals.

were celebrated in paintings and prose. Local breeds and varieties were still to be found on farms – red Devon cattle, brown and white Herefords – but to an increasing extent, farmers were cross-breeding local strains with animals more common elsewhere, or were putting their money into more 'efficient' breeds. Thus, the English long-horn cattle became dominant in areas where cattle were being raised for meat, but were superseded at the end of the century by more manageable short-horn varieties like the Hereford. Among dairy cattle, the Friesian, which had been introduced to England in the 1860s, began to carry all before it. As with cattle, so with sheep and pigs: breeding experiments produced animals with better characteristics for meat or wool production, and older, often very local varieties of animals began to disappear.

Among the farm tasks was milking, which was often done in the fields. In Thomas Hardy's *Tess of the D'Urbervilles*, there is a memorable scene of all the farm hands out in the early morning with their stools and pails. The milk was collected and, by the later nineteenth century, in many areas it was taken to the railway station to go on the milk train to some large urban centre.

Two engravings from William Youatt's The Complete Grazier, and Farmer and Cattle-breeder's Assistant. *Of the Sussex cow* (above) *he writes, 'few of the cows are good milkers, the breed is a great favourite with the butchers, second to none as regards early maturity and weight for age'; and of the Hereford bull* (right), *'the eye is full . . . denoting the quietness of disposition and temper . . . which is of paramount importance to ensure the profitable feeding of all ruminating animals.'*

Usually in the spring or early summer, the calves would be born. Autumn might see the slaughter of the beasts, as the weaker animals were weeded out before the winter came. Sheep might be sent on to higher pastures or brought down; in the spring they would lamb, in the summer they would be dipped and their fleeces shorn.

Then there were the horses. Although oxen survived as beasts of power and burden in a few parts of the country, in the nineteenth century they were almost entirely replaced by horses. Horses pulled the ploughs and the early reaping machines in the harvest fields, walked in circles driving grinding wheels in mills; they were harnessed to wagons and carts, to bring in hay or the harvested wheat, to take produce to market or to deliver on a farm round. A horse would pull the farmer and his wife in their carriage or be ridden to hounds. No farm, however small, could do without its horse. By the end of the last century, there were millions of horses in England, of which the largest number by far were working farm horses. Steam and many other forms of power were still to be accepted on many of the farms in the English countryside.

Power on the land: Youatt describes the mule (left) as being cheaper to maintain than a horse, and with the donkey a useful animal for the smallholder; and the Old English black carthorse (above) as one of the strongest of all draught animals, used wherever heavy pulling or roadwork is required.

WORKING THE LAND

'Seed Time', dated 1854, by John Frederick Herring. A farm worker guides the plough and, beyond, a team of horses pulls a roller. Perhaps to point to new developments in farming, the artist included a man broad-casting seed in the manner unchanged since medieval times.

WHEREAS THE FARM WORKER in the fields is a rare and solitary sight today, in the early Victorian countryside the fields might be busy with people all year round. Only late in the century, when livestock became more important in England's rural economy and machinery began to make its presence felt, did field work begin to play a less prominent part in the business of farming. Staffordshire pottery mugs often still carried this traditional verse:

O happy is the farmer and free from all care
Who rises every morning to breathe fresh air
And hears the bird's singing from every green bough.

The harvest fields at Radford in Warwickshire by Thomas Baker of Leamington. The ripe corn has been stooked, waiting to be taken by cart to the stackyard. In the distance stands a large country house, almost matched in size by the huge stack of corn which has already been brought in.

No life like the farmer's that follows the plough.
Success e'er attend him and plenty and peace
May the seeds that he sows with blessings increase
May health still around him its comforts bestow
Long life to the farmer and God speed the plough.

The farm year began just before or just after Christmas with the preparation of the ground, when furrows were cut and the soil was turned with the plough. As the nineteenth century progressed, so the design of ploughs advanced, giving greater speed and depth of tillage. The old wrought-iron ploughshare made by local carpenters and blacksmiths was replaced by one in 'chilled' cast iron, manufactured by a process perfected by Ransomes of Ipswich, a firm that came to dominate the nineteenth-century agricultural machinery trade.

The plough was drawn by a pair or a team of horses. Almost nowhere did oxen draw ploughs in the nineteenth century; but occasionally, still, on smallholdings and the poorest upland farms, fields were prepared with a breast plough, which a man pushed into the land rather than having it drawn by beasts.

Ploughing was a skill, one in which particular pride was taken. Ploughmen could be discovered strolling out on a Sunday to cast a critical eye over the fields of neighbouring farms, and they would take part in ploughing matches at country fairs and shows. A good furrow had to be straight as a die, and the overall effect as tidy as might be. One Yorkshire lad at the turn of the century recalled being set to plough with two horses 'and a more ill-assorted pair it would be hard to imagine. Short was a ready-going old plodder, while Betsey the trap mare was eager to be going, and Short's steady pace irritated her till she went wild with excitement. . . I was neither big enough nor strong enough to turn the plough on the headland and the trap mare would keep getting a leg over the chains when turning at the ends. Then round she would spin, kicking and jumping; over would go the plough, with me clinging on and ready to cry for vexation.'

'Building the Hay-Rick', one of Myles Birket Foster's 'Pictures of English Landscape' published in 1863. Tom Taylor's accompanying poem savoured the event, 'The heavy hay-piled wains roll in . . . / Till all the air for miles away / Breathes of fresh and fragrant hay.'

The most significant development was the introduction of the steam plough from the 1860s – which was not a steam engine pulling a plough behind it, but steam engines set on either side of a field, with a wire between them, along which the plough travelled. Such equipment was too costly for a single farm to have, and so at the end of the last century came travelling engines with a team of men and ploughs, which were hired out by the day. It was an exciting sight, speed and smoke replacing the long, patient tread of horse and man.

After ploughing, the land was further prepared by harrowing, to level the ground, stir up the soil and break up clods of earth. In the unforgettable lines by Thomas Hardy:

> Only a man harrowing clods
> In a slow silent walk
> With an old horse that stumbles and nods
> Half asleep as they stalk.

A watercolour by J. A. Atkinson of haymakers. It was maybe an idealistic Tom Taylor who wrote, 'Happy, hot, haymaking time, | Heart of the glad summer's prime, | When even labour seems in tune, | For once, with joys of balmy June; | When freely flows the farmer's beer, | And toil shakes hands with lusty cheer.'

The oldest form of harrow – which observers were surprised to find was still being used in nineteenth-century Dorset – was a thorn bush weighted down by a log, and pulled by a draught animal. Most Victorian harrows were heavy, spiked frames that were made for the purpose; by the 1840s the zig-zag harrow still in use today began to make its appearance.

Children were employed to pick stones, and gradually the field was made ready for sowing seed: wheat, oats or barley, clover, root vegetables, potatoes or beans, or some other commercial crop such as woad, a dye-plant. The traditional method of sowing seed by broad-cast, with a walking man scattering seed from a bag, continued, but increasingly the job was done by machinery. Seed drills incorporated a hopper, from which seed fell into a shallow furrow made by a press wheel, and then an attached brush would cover over the seed, or else that would be done manually.

Then the weeds began to grow: the bane of the women and children who were commonly employed in the back-breaking task of keeping the fields free of thistles, docks, nettles and ox-eyes, hoeing or pulling by hand.

In early summer, haymaking – called 'haysel' in some parts of the country – occupied the farm hands, and often many of the village men and women who at most times of the year had other jobs. Haymaking was often portrayed as a happy, leisurely activity, with country people basking in the warmth of the June sun, and so it often proved to be; but there were always anxieties about the weather holding.

The grass was mown, most often with a long-handled scythe, by men moving in long lines through the grass, and once cut it lay in the fields to dry. If green hay were to be stacked, it could lead to spontaneous combustion. In Miss Mitford's village, Farmer Bridgwater 'set six men on to mowing a little after sunrise, and collected fourteen efficient haymakers by breakfast-time. Fourteen active haymakers for our poor three acres! Not to count the idle assistants; we ourselves, with three dogs and two boys to mind them, advisers who came to find fault and look on, babies who came to be nursed, children who came to rock the babies, and other children who came to keep the rockers company and play with the dogs; to say nothing of this small rabble, we had fourteen able-bodied men and women in one hay-field, besides the six

'Life in a Hop Field', a bucolic scene painted by Phoebus Levin. Babies sleep protected from the September sun, while their mothers strip the flowers from the bines. Beyond are the high roofs and cowls of the oast houses where the hops were dried. 'Foreign' pickers would come from the towns to help the locals.

mowers, who had got the grass down by noon, and, finding the strong beer good and plentiful, magnanimously volunteered to stay and help get in the crop.'

The hay had to be turned by hand every few days; then wide wooden rakes, often wielded by the women of the village, were used to pull the hay into cocks, which were later carted away and built into a stack. At each stage, bad weather could harm or even ruin the hay, and only when the stack, or rick, had been built, and a thatched roof (or later a tarpaulin) fixed over it, could the farmer and his men breathe a sigh of relief.

The harvest was an immense activity. The entire neighbourhood was involved, from farmers to itinerant workers, from fit men and their wives to their children and aged parents. The harvest in mid-Victorian England involved more workers than at any previous time.

The four basic harvesting tools were all hand tools: the sickle, the reaping hook, the fagging hook and the scythe. All the crops of the summer harvests – hay in June and July, peas at the end of July, corn in August, and hops in September – were, at least until the mid-century, cut and stacked by hand.

When harvest time arrived, most of the villagers migrated to the cornfields. For every eight acres of wheat ready for cutting there would generally be eight men engaged on the task. They might draw lots for their strips in the field, and then eight families would begin to drive their pathway into the standing corn. Remembering his Berkshire upbringing, J. G. Cornish described the scene in the 1880s: 'Father with his broad-bladed fagging hook in his right hand and crooked stick in his left, slashed through the yellow stalks and left them gathered by his foot. Mother followed, swept a sheaf together, placed it on the "bond", drew this tightly and fastened it by the twist. The children pulled the bonds, the younger perhaps only able to select six or eight stalks needed to make one, the elder making them ready for mother to use.'

In the fight against time and the weather to bring in the crops, occupational barriers that existed at other times of the year came down. The carpenters and wheelwrights left their benches, the masons laid down their trowels. If they had not gone to help in the harvest, the farmers would have withheld their patronage during the winter. All 'sizes and ages, men and women, Irish and English,

Two different forms of scythe; each region evolved its own particular pattern for the implements made by the local blacksmith.

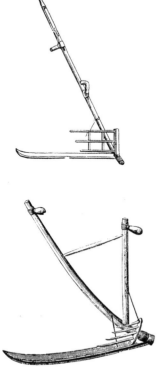

Reaping corn with a scythe, which was faster than working with the sickle used in earlier centuries. To cut the corn at the optimum moment, as many reapers as possible would be called in to work.

strollers and neighbours, reapers and faggers, good workmen and bad, grandmothers and children, kettle-boilers and tiers, married and single' formed the throng on the fields, as Tom Strong described in *Stubble Farm*. It was a true community of work.

Every task was urgent. Once cut, the corn could not stand unsheaved overnight; and, in turn, ripe corn could not stand in sheaves for long before the ears began to shed. The sheer amount of work to be done meant that village labour was supplemented by bands of roving harvest workers, who moved from parish to parish during the season, many coming from Ireland, some from towns; some were simply footloose countrymen. As Gerard Manley Hopkins described in 'Hurraing in Harvest', in 1877:

> Summer ends now; now, barbarous in beauty, the stooks rise
> Around; up above, what wind-walks! what lovely behaviour
> Of silk-sack clouds! has wider, wilful-wavier
> Meal-drift moulded ever and melted across skies?

This had been the pattern from time immemorial. Yet change was in the air. Firstly, the women no longer harvested directly alongside the men in the way they had done in previous centuries. Victorian sensibilities pushed them back into the second row of work. The supply of labour in the countryside began to dry up, as

When the oats or barley were cut wet the sheaf might be 'gaited', that is set up to stand on its own. Usually sheaves were set in stooks, groups of sheaves propped up against each other.

A reaping machine devised by the Reverend Patrick Bell in the 1820s but illustrated by Loudon in his Encyclopedia of Agriculture of 1844. However, it was not until the 1860s that machines were developed which left the cut corn to the side of the machine, and the 1870s that a self-binding reaper became available. These inventions were a blessing to the farmer, who was by then finding it increasingly difficult to employ enough labour at harvest time.

people left the land, and by the 1860s and 1870s machine harvesting was beginning to make an impact upon the countryside: the machine mower and the machine reaper with its painted 'sails'.

This brought a new rhythm to the harvest: large groups were in thrall to the machine, stacking and carting away what it cut at a fast rate. There was less work for travelling harvesters, and consequently less of the raucous fun they brought to the village. Yet, even by the 1890s, probably only one farm in a hundred had a mechanical reaper; although farmers might borrow each others' equipment or employ contract machinery, hand harvesting continued alongside the machine well into the present century.

Richard Jefferies reminded his readers how physical the work of the Victorian harvester was: 'Your skin or mine,' he told them, 'could not have stood the scratching of the straw, which is stiff and sharp, and the burning of the sun, which blisters like red-hot iron. No one could stand the harvest-field as a reaper except he had been born' to it. The goal was a good yield, corn to sell and corn to grind, and the merrymaking that went with the harvest home.

'The women and children swarmed over the stubble picking up the ears of wheat the horse-rake had missed. Up and down and over and over the stubble they hurried, backs bent, eyes on the ground, one hand outstretched to pick up the ears, the other resting on the small of the back with the "handful"... the single ears mounted, and a woman with four or five strong, well-disciplined children would carry a good load home on her head every night.' As Flora Thompson described in *Lark Rise to Candleford*, it had always been the custom that, after the harvest had been safely brought in, women and children from the village were allowed into the fields to glean, that is, to pick up the fallen grains that the harvesters had missed. Gleaning provided the wheat grains for the flour on which many poorer families depended, and barley grains to feed the chickens and the cottage pig.

A bell would often be rung, to signal that gleaning could commence. In some places, the elderly or those on poor relief were allowed to go over the field first, but elsewhere it was a free-for-all. Gleaning was seen as one of the traditional rights of the poor.

As soon as the harvest was gathered in, the next stage, of preparing the grain, began: this was threshing, to remove the chaff and the husk. The earliest advances in mechanized farming took place

Laying hedges and repairing fences to make them stock-proof was important winter and spring work in an era before barbed wire. The hedger's children bring him food and drink in this painting by John Brett.

in threshing, which had been one of the most back-breaking of all farming tasks. Traditionally, threshing was carried out by hand, using a flail on a pile of grain on a barn floor, where huge open doors on either side produced a through draught which blew the lighter chaff away, leaving the heavier grain to fall back to the floor. On farms growing grain on a large scale, threshing must have seemed a never-ending task, especially since it was usually done on dark, cold, winter days. Yet the early threshing machines, driven by water and then by steam, were at first vigorously resisted by farm workers, especially in southern and eastern England, since threshing provided much-needed winter work.

Machine power won the day, and after the middle of the nineteenth century the flail became an ever-rarer sight, the steam engine with threshing machine attached ever more common. Hardy's Tess was placed upon the threshing machine at Flintcomb-Ash Farm, 'her business being to untie every sheaf of corn handed on to her by Izz Huett, who stood next, but on the rick; so that the feeder [man] could seize it and spread it over the revolving drum, which whisked out every grain in a moment'. It was a day's hard work of sweat and toil, with 'the red tyrant that the women had come to serve – a timber-framed construction, with straps and wheels appertaining – the threshing machine which, whilst it was going, kept up a despotic demand upon the endurance of their muscles and nerves'.

Winter was a period when work was slacker, and then the farmer and his labourers would use their time to do all those farm tasks that seemed to get left undone when everyone was busy. Hedges needed cutting and laying, ditches needed scouring; new drainage pipes were always required to make the fields more productive. Weeds and stones occupied the farm worker and his family at whatever time of the year.

One of the most important crops on many of the Victorian farms were the mangels, turnips and swedes, which provided food for the sheep, pigs and cattle. Digging the root crops, preparing

Turnip sowing machine or hand drill (above) illustrated in William Youatt's The Complete Grazier *of 1877.*

A corn and seed drill (left) manufactured by Messrs Garrett & Son of Saxmundham, Suffolk. During the mid-nineteenth century rapid improvements were made in seed drills and each manufacturer patented his own refinements.

An example published in 1877 of the latest step in the mechanization of agriculture: a double-engine system of steam ploughing, involving power from two traction engines pulling a plough along a hawser from either end of the field.

clamps, where they could be stored in the fields away from frost until they were needed, and trimming and cutting up the roots, were all autumn and winter tasks. Women especially were employed for the turnips, and all found it hard work. Just as Tess of the D'Urbervilles had been overheated at the threshing machine, so she was near-frozen at turnip trimming. 'At this occupation', she and her friend Marian 'could shelter themselves by a thatched hurdle if it rained; but if it was frosty even their thick leather gloves could not prevent the frozen masses they handled from biting their fingers.'

There was also work to be done on the other animals' feedstuffs. A chaffcutter, which cut straw and hay into shorter lengths, was the principal piece of equipment used in making the feed for horses. James Caird described what he saw on Yorkshire farms in 1850. In winter, the farm horses 'were fed on a mixture of oat and wheat straw, and a small portion of clover hay, cut together into chaff. This is placed in the horses' manger, and then slightly damped with water, after which about a quart of bean meal is strewn over it, which, being well mixed by hand, adheres to the wet chaff, and makes the whole a palatable and nutritious feed for the farm horse.' The needs of plants and animals never ceased in the farmer's annual round.

'The Farmer's Friend' produced by Messrs Howard of Bedford, illustrated and described in a farming manual of 1877, 'by a very ingenious combination of arrangements it can be made serviceable in a number of ways: as a traction engine or a self-propelling engine; a steam cultivation engine; and by taking away the windlass used for this it may be employed at the homestead for thrashing grain, or for working various machines.'

CHAPTER 4
CRAFTS AND TRADES

VILLAGE CRAFTSMEN

'VILLAGES USED TO CONTAIN, in addition to the agricultural inhabitants,' wrote Thomas Hardy late in the nineteenth century, 'an interesting and better-informed class, ranking distinctly above [the other inhabitants] – the blacksmith, the carpenter, the shoemaker, the small higgler, the shopkeeper.' A range of different craftsmen was needed to maintain the village and many of the larger villages would have been virtually self-sufficient, especially in the days before factory mass-production of machinery and clothing.

The 'prince of the tradesmen', as he has been called – usually the strongest man in the community and as such noted for his usefulness on the cricket pitch – was the blacksmith. Longfellow provided an enduring image of the village blacksmith at work:

> Week in, week out, from morn till night
> You can hear his bellows blow;
> You can hear him swing his heavy sledge,
> With measured beat and slow,
> Like a sexton ringing a village bell,
> When the evening sun is low.

All sorts of agricultural machinery and implements, the iron fittings for farm carts and wagons, including the metal rims on the wheels that served as tyres, the iron hinges and locks for doors and windows in cottages and farmhouses, and, in particular, shoes for the horses, were produced in the heat of the blacksmith's shop, to the accompaniment of the roar of bellows and the ring of hammer on anvil.

A Hertfordshire blacksmith recalled the trade in his village at the end of the century: 'I sharpened bill-hooks, scythes, sickles, axes, and every type of edged tool, often replacing the broken or split staves and stales. I made pitchforks and four-tined ploughs,

John Hill, the painter of this picture, was a carpenter, as was his father. The workshop depicted here in fine detail probably belonged to one or other of them, at Forty Hill in Enfield, Middlesex. The stout paper hats folded into a box-like shape were traditionally worn by plasterers and house-painters as well as carpenters.

plough spuds, coulters, shears, drills and harrows; sometimes renewing the entire set of teeth on worn-out harrows.' Labourers came to him with their special needs – for a left-handed scythe or one with a longer blade for a man with big arms – while both gamekeepers and poachers asked for long curved spades to dig out rabbits and ferrets. In a larger village or on an estate there might have been found a farrier, whose particular trade it was to shoe horses (and often doctor them as well), but most villages had to manage with a single smith. He was kept in business by the sheer number of horses in the countryside – over a million horses were used in agriculture at the end of Queen Victoria's reign, as well as a very considerable number of carriage horses and horses and ponies for riding. All needed shoeing, and a working horse might need to be shod every few weeks.

The wheelwright, who usually doubled as wainwright, was also an essential craftsman in any village. His was the specialized task of making for the horse-drawn farm carts and wagons their wheels with wooden stocks and spokes, and repairing them. Every locality had its own particular type of cart, the product of local requirements and traditions, sometimes gaily painted in a style peculiar to a small knot of villages. George Sturt, who ran a wheelwright's business in Farnham, Surrey, from the 1880s, was the third generation to enter the trade, providing for the varied needs of the vicinity: 'In farm-wagon or dung-cart, barley-roller, plough,

Early nineteenth-century engravings of the wheelwright's craft; a pivotal figure in the neighbourhood, he created the wheels for every kind of cart, wagon and barrow. (Above) morticing the spokes on to the stock, always an even number; (below) fitting the wheel on to the cart.

water-barrel or whatnot, the dimensions we chose, the curves we followed (and almost every piece of timber was curved) were imposed upon us by the nature of the soil in this or that farm, the gradient of this or that hill, the temper of this or that customer or his choice perhaps in horseflesh...'

The wheelwright needed to know all the woods of the neighbourhood, and to be able to choose the right pieces of timber when trees were felled. Each stock and each spoke was a hand-crafted item of beauty, the driving of the spokes into the wheel a delicate operation of the greatest accuracy which yet required a sledge hammer to effect.

Also dealing in wood was the village carpenter, but his was a much less specialized craft. When Sol, a carpenter who appears in Hardy's *The Hand of Ethelberta*, wanted to move to London, he was advised to restrict the number of things he claimed to be able to do, otherwise he would not succeed. In his home village, he was quite happy to turn his hand to any task that was needed: he was 'a very good staircase hand, neat at sash frames, can knock together doors and shutters very well... and can do a little at the cabinet-making'. He would make a roof when required, and spent any spare time he had 'at planing floor-boards by the foot'.

As with the wheelwright, the carpenter's skill also lay in knowing what timber to use and how to saw and season it. Some were also woodsmen, felling trees and sawing timber in the sawpits. The

George Sturt, a wheelwright in Farnham, described his business at the end of the century, 'There was no looking far afield for customers. Farmers rarely lived more than five miles away; millers, brewers, a local grocer or builder or timber-merchant or hop-grower – for such and no other did the ancient shop cater, as it had done for nearly two centuries.'

carpenter might double as cooper, making wooden barrels for brewing, for use as water butts or for carrying milk. And the basic wooden furniture in the farm cottages was likewise made by him. He would often mix simple traditional forms with a motif or detail fashionable at some earlier time or associated with a grander style of furniture. The building and restoration work carried out on country houses and churches in Victorian times gave employment to village craftsmen such as the carpenters, and it might introduce them to new techniques and styles.

Hardy, who mentions many of the country crafts in his novels, came from a family of house builders and masons in the villages near Dorchester, starting with his grandfather, a jobbing mason on his own, and ending with his brother who employed a dozen or so men as masons and labourers. Local vernacular traditions survived in cottage and farm building, although the pattern books and the architectural fancies of landowners building model villages and farms gradually became known in the countryside.

In some parts of the country, such as Sussex, there was a tradition of brick-making and of building using timber, both as framing and for weatherboarding. In Devon and Dorset, many of the cottages and farm buildings were built in cob, made from earth, clay, chalk, straw, dung and whatever else might be to hand; claylump

A cooper's workshop, painted by Joseph Wrightson McIntyre in 1877. The planks would have been cut in a sawpit in the age-old manner if there was no local sawmill. A variety of casks, barrels, pails and tubs for use in the kitchen, dairy and brewery were made by the village cooper. He would generally use oak for the staves and ash, hazel, or indeed iron, for the hoops.

The smith, perhaps the most important craftsman in the village, in a painting by Edwin F. Holt. Wearing his traditional red hat, the smith works the bellows for the forge, while the farrier shoes the cob. In the foreground is the anvil on which the horseshoes are hammered into shape.

Two craftsmen common in sheep-rearing areas: (above) the woolcomber and (below) the weaver. Weavers' cottages could be identified by the extra-large window openings which gave the weaver maximum light at his loom.

walls were used for fenland cottages in the eastern counties, while in the villages of Northamptonshire and in other places where stone was plentiful, cottages and farms were built of stone, and masons were employed in building and in repair work. The more humble buildings would be in rough or rubble walling; the larger cottages and houses in dressed freestone.

Thatch was an important roofing material in some parts of the country, especially in places with mud-walled houses, where a considerable overhang of thatch kept rainwater from running down the walls. Ricks were usually thatched after the harvest, since a good waterproof cover was needed to prevent the corn from becoming sodden in the autumn rains. The thatcher and his boy were familiar figures in villages across England, with their ladders, their long bundles of straw or reed, and the spars, usually of twisted hazel, which held the thatch in place. Damp weather was best for thatching, for then the straw worked in closely together; it became brittle in a frost or when it was hot. Stewart Dick described the procedure: 'When the straw is laid on, it is combed or raked down to make it smooth. The old thatcher's rake was a most primitive instrument, consisting merely of a stout ash rod with a number of large nails driven through it to form the teeth. After being combed down, the thatch is trimmed with a flat knife mounted on a handle like that of a builder's trowel. The eaves are then cut square with a hook like a reaping-hook, and finished off with shears.' Straw that had been machine reaped was bruised and lasted for only a third as long as straw reaped by hand.

Elsewhere, clay tiles or split stone tiles were used, the latter needing a very sturdy roof structure to support the weight. As the nineteenth century progressed, so village builders needed to adapt their techniques to the new materials that were spreading across the country: bricks that were made in large brickyards in the clay-lands of eastern and central England, and slate quarried in north Wales. Their durability and availability served to diminish the individual character of the vernacular architecture in many re-gions, and house builders' specialized local skills began to decline.

Tanners and saddlers had their place in the community, and shoe and bootmakers were to be found everywhere in Victorian England. The cobbler's workshop was a favourite gathering place in the village. The village choir in Hardy's *Under the Greenwood*

(Above) *The basket-maker, who usually plied his craft near the osier or withy beds of low-lying river land; (below) the saddler and harness-maker without whom no horse could be worked or ridden.*

Tree met outside Penny the shoemaker's, where Mr Penny would sit 'facing the road with a boot on his knees and the awl in his hand', and a taciturn apprentice who 'smiled at remarks that floated in from without, but was never known to answer them in Mr Penny's presence'.

A country tradesman serving the craftsmen and all the people of the village was the carrier. The country carrier provided many rural communities with their main link to the world outside. In the 1880s, at least 20,000 rural carriers plied the roads, their horse-drawn carts loaded with goods and – like Barkis, who was willing for Peggotty in *David Copperfield* – taking passengers cheaply, if painfully slowly, from place to place. The Cambridgeshire village carriers on their way into the market towns used to take 'commissions all along the road – a packet of needles for Mrs This, and a new teapot for Mrs That – and delivered them all correctly on the way back', depositing passengers as they went. As one Yorkshireman remembered: 'In one thing could the carrier's cart beat the modern 'bus, and that was in the variety of smells. There was tarpaulin over all; then came leather, then apples and cow cake, with occasionally a calf or a crate of chickens. We lurched and rolled steadily along, without much thought of time or speed, until we entered the first village on the road to town, where old Jasper, the blue-roan horse, drew up from force of habit in front of the Little Brown Jug.' There were always country jokes – and *Punch* cartoons – about pedestrians overtaking the carrier, but his cart was a lifeline for the general population in rural areas.

The march of progress, and the decline in the rural population, meant that many of these village crafts and trades would wither away. The coming of steam and then the internal combustion engine, and the decline in the use of the working horse, meant that trades such as the blacksmith's had to adapt or die. Blacksmith's shops became bicycle repair shops and then garages, and George Sturt's wheelwrights' company was eventually to be sold to a car bodymaker.

The shoemaker or cordwainer. He might supply boots to the farmer made from leather supplied by the village tanner, who in turn used the hides of the farmer's slaughtered animals.

THE MILL

THE CORN MILL IN Thomas Hardy's novel, *The Trumpet-Major*, 'presented at one end the appearance of a hard-worked house slipping into the river, and at the other of an idle, genteel place, half-cloaked with creepers... [It had] two mill doors, one above the other, the upper enabling a person to step out upon nothing at a height of ten feet from the ground; a gaping arch vomiting the river... In the court at the front were two worn-out millstones, made useful again by being let in level with the ground. Here people stood to smoke and consider things in muddy weather; and cats slept on the clean surfaces when it was hot.' Inside, a fine mist of flour gave a pallid look to every surface, and the building was filled 'morning, noon, and night by the music of the mill, the wheels and cogs of which, being of wood, produced notes that might have borne in their minds a remote resemblance to the wooden tones of the stopped diapason in an organ. Occasionally, when the miller was bolting, there was added to these continuous sounds the cheerful clicking of the hopper'.

Mills driven by water and high-standing windmills with their fan-tails and great inclined sails were features of the early Victorian countryside. Farmers brought grain to the mills in sackloads, to be ground and sent to market, and cottage families brought the small quantities they had acquired through gleaning in the fields at the end of the harvest.

The miller was a local character, and in England in 1851 there were over 37,000. The opportunity for sharp practice – producing less weight of flour than was brought in corn, or substituting good meal with bad – meant that he was not always trusted; and his charges were often cause for complaint. Traces of the flour and dust that clung to him from head to toe – even when dressed in his best clothes – made him easy to recognize.

The mill was vital to the village economy, for every household needed flour to make the bread that formed a staple part of the diet. Since milling had been a right restricted to the lord of the manor, and owning a hand mill illegal, there was not much of a tradition of grinding corn at home. The millpond and the

A watermill at Coniston with an overshot wheel, painted by John Henry Mole. In the Lake District there was no shortage of water to drive the great wooden wheels of the mills. Farmers sent sackloads of corn to be ground, while the villagers brought small amounts, often gleaned from the fields at the end of the harvest.

waterwheel, and the windmill's sails quivering or turning in the breeze, were sights that had been common for centuries. As the following lines, written to accompany one of Myles Birket Foster's engravings, expressed it, the mill was:

> In its place upon the hill –
> Sweeping sails or standing still –
> Emblem of enduring will.
> Serving with a constant mind,
> Though it serve the inconstant wind.

Of the two types, watermills were the more ancient, and several thousand of them are recorded in the Domesday Book. The way the waterwheel was worked, either with an undershot form in which the wheel sat on the water and was turned by the flow, or the more efficient overshot wheel where the water was brought from above, was governed by the type of river or millpond that was available. The need for a ready and constant flow of water often required the construction of a complicated system of ponds, weirs and water courses.

Windmills had made their appearance in England in the twelfth century. The earliest were post mills, the whole body of the mill turning to catch the wind. They were superseded by smock mills, constructed so that the cap carrying the sails turned and the body remained fixed. Many were built at the end of the eighteenth century and through the nineteenth, as the wind often blew more readily than the water's flow could be tamed, but that depended, of course, on the lie of the land. In both windmills and watermills, a series of gears and shafts drove the great millstones that ground the corn into flour. The sharp edges on the stone cut the corn, and shallow grooves carried the flour.

Some villages and small towns had a maltings – often attached to a mill – where barley was malted for use in beer-making and in animal feed. Warren's malthouse in Hardy's *Far from the Madding Crowd* was a typical example. It had a steeply pitched roof topped by a lantern vented by louvres on all four sides, 'and from these openings a mist was dimly perceived to be escaping into the night air. There was no window in front; but a square hole in the door was glazed with a single pane, through which red, comfortable rays now stretched out...' Inside, everything was permeated with the

(Left) *Three different designs of windmill, engraved in the early nineteenth century. The most basic type, the post mill (bottom) carried the sails on a post and the entire structure would be turned to face the wind. The tower, smock or frock mill (top and centre) was an improvement on this whereby the sails were held on a revolving cap. William Cobbett described the inconvenience of trips to the miller, 'sometimes the water fails and sometimes the wind. Many a farmer's wife has been tempted to vent her spleen on both. At best there must be horse and man or boy and, perhaps, cart to go to the mill.'*

sweet smell of new malt as the barley was heated. In hop-growing areas, especially in Kent and eastern parts of Sussex, the distinctive oasthouses, with their cowls that turned to catch the wind, were used for drying hops that were the other essential ingredient in beer-making. The old, square, brick or wood buildings were often replaced in the Victorian period by round oasthouses.

In areas of grain or hop production, all roads seemed to lead to the place where the crops were converted into the basics of food and drink – and into money. In Hardy's 'The Second Visit':

> Clack, clack, clack, went the mill-wheel as I came,
> And she was on the bridge with the thin hand-rail,
> And the miller at the door, and the ducks at mill-tail;
> I come again years after, and all there seems the same.

Yet all that was there was not to be the same for ever. The windmills and the waterwheels gradually stopped turning as steam-powered mills, with rollers rather than wheels, started to process the hard wheat grain that was coming in from America and Canada in the later nineteenth century. Home-grown grain was more likely to be sold further afield, and to be milled by the big flour companies in mills driven by steam and later by oil. From being everywhere, mills and maltings began to disappear from villages, and to be concentrated in the large towns and the ports.

The dusty miller, the 'bulging fifteen-stone man' who was the proprietor of Hardy's Overcombe Mill, ceased to be the conspicuous member of the community that he had once been. But, for years to come, behind the mill door would be visible the 'chalked addition and subtraction sums, many of them originally done wrong, and the figures half rubbed out and corrected, noughts being turned into nines, and ones into twos'. These had been the miller's private calculations of loads ground and customers outwitted.

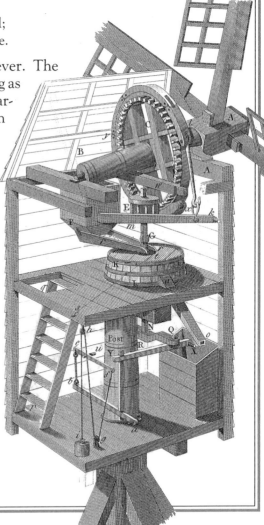

Diagram showing the workings of a windmill, a feature of the English landscape since the twelfth century. Many refinements were made during the eighteenth century: fantails were introduced, the gearings were made of cast iron and the millstones could be more precisely gauged.

THE RIVER

FEW VILLAGES WERE WITHOUT access to some river or stream; indeed, the watercourse was often the reason for a village's very existence. As a local watercourse changed course or dried up, some English villages, such as Kidlington in Oxfordshire, were abandoned and rebuilt only a short distance away several times in the course of their history. Many village place names derive from rivers – some, like the Winterbourne villages in Dorset and Wiltshire, reflecting the fact that the water flow was seasonal. Charles Kingsley's affectionate portrait of the river in *The Water-Babies* summons up the charms of running water:

> Clear and cool, clear and cool,
> By laughing shallow, and dreaming pool;
> Cool and clear, cool and clear,
> By shining shingle, and foaming weir.

A painting by Myles Birket Foster of men pushing their boat out into the river to set eel traps. The simplest traps were made from a sack fitted to a drain pipe, filled with straw and baited with offal; more efficient traps, like these, were made of wicker.

Under the crag where the ouzel sings,
And the ivied wall where the church-bell rings,
Undefiled, for the undefiled;
Play by me, bathe in me, mother and child.

The river provided water for washing and bathing, for watering the cattle, for fishing and for play. Water attracted children, who spent happy summer days paddling and catching minnows, while their parents might cool off in the river after long, hot days in the harvest fields.

The river stood for the happier side of country life. In the last days before the First World War, in which he was to die, Edward Thomas wrote of being:

Seated once by a brook, watching a child
Chiefly that paddled, I was thus beguiled.
Mellow the blackbird sang and sharp the thrush
Not far off in the oak and hazel brush,
Unseen. There was a scent like honeycomb

Gathering watercress on the River Mole in Surrey, a painting by William Frederick Witherington. Children were sent to search for watercress, mushrooms, blackberries and other food that grew wild in the countryside.

From mugwort dull. And down upon the dome
Of the stone the cart-horse kicks against so oft
A butterfly alighted.

Fishing was one of the pleasures of rural life. William Howitt began his chapter on midsummer in the fields: 'I never see a clear stream running through the fields at this beautiful time of year but I wish, like old Isaak Walton, to take up rod and line.' The Victorians read and relished Walton's *The Compleat Angler*, with its classic observations on fishing.

For Howitt and his like, fishing was a sport, and on country estates the fish were as carefully guarded against poachers as any game bird. Fly fishing was for the gentry, while townspeople on a day out in the country used a rod and line with hook and bait to catch bream and chub and other freshwater fish, including the barbel which was reputed to live only in rivers flowing from west to east. The local people fished mainly for food. Traps made of withies were set for eels, or night-lines were baited and set up on the river banks. With bobbing, forty or fifty worms were threaded on to a line and the rod flicked up and down until a bite was felt on it.

The river was also essential to some types of work. It powered the mills that ground the corn, and the new mills in which cotton and wool were spun and cloth was woven. River water was needed, too, for the older industrial processes such as tanning and dyeing. Watercress grew in the cleaner streams, and was taken to town to sell. Wherever there were willow beds, in the damp ground beside rivers, withy or osier peeling was a local industry. The baskets made from the withies were usually produced nearby. This was an important local craft in Berkshire and Surrey, and at

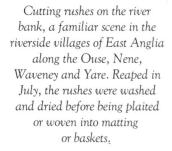

Cutting rushes on the river bank, a familiar scene in the riverside villages of East Anglia along the Ouse, Nene, Waveney and Yare. Reaped in July, the rushes were washed and dried before being plaited or woven into matting or baskets.

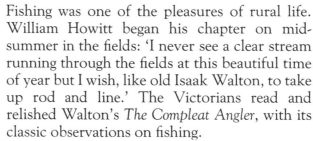

(Below, left to right) Salmon, gudgeon and trout, engraved for The Practical Fisherman *by J. H. Keene, published in 1881. The gudgeon was delicious, 'if cooked as the Thames-side fishermen's wives know how'.*

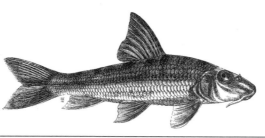

other places on the banks of the Thames close to the market gardens that served London; also in Lincolnshire, in the southern parts of Derbyshire and in areas such as Sedgemoor in the Somerset Levels. An employer whose business was on the banks of the River Dove, in Derbyshire, described in the late 1860s how the peeling season ran from the end of April to June, when 'I can employ all the hands I can get, women and children, mothers bring their babies in cradles with them, whole families work together, the mother breaks the peel (draws the willow through a 'brake'), and the children peel.' The peel itself was used to tie up the bundles of osiers or dried for use as kindling. Larger poles were used for fencing and staking, and in a few places willow was reserved for making cricket bats; but it was basketwork that this localized craft principally served. A great number of baskets and hampers were used, in the house and in the garden, and for transporting merchandise, and there was always a demand for them.

Working rivercraft carried goods and ferried passengers where there was no bridge and where the water was too deep for a ford. The economy of some parts of the country – the fens of East Anglia and the wetlands of Somerset – depended on water for fishing and fowling, for clays from the riverbed, and reeds and sedge which were used for roofing. In the Victorian period the use of boats was the only means of bringing goods into these low-lying communities and taking out the local produce. Even when the railway extended all over the country, rivers and the canal networks they fed into were still carrying a massive volume of trade.

The river was, to an extent that is almost forgotten, one of the great resources of the Victorian countryside.

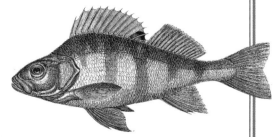

An engraving entitled 'Trolling for Jack'. Trolling meant using a spinner as a lure and a jack was another name for the pike. J. H. Keene described this fish as 'an agreeable addition to the table of the poor at least'.

(Below, left to right) The grayling, pike and perch. Keene's suggested bait (following Izaak Walton) was a grasshopper or cricket for the first, a live frog for the second and a minnow for the third.

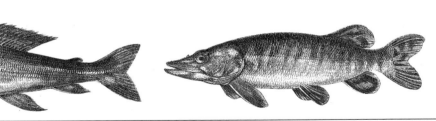

THE WOOD

THOMAS HARDY GREW UP IN a green and leafy world in the 1840s and 1850s, his family home a part of the long history of building in woodland clearings and on poor and waste land. In these lines, from his first published poem, Hardy described his birthplace, his 'Domicilium', which stands still among the woods at Higher Bockhampton in Dorset:

> It faces west, and round the back and sides
> High beeches, bending, hang a veil of boughs,
> And sweep against the roof.

Woodlands were an integral part of the English countryside.

When the wars with France came to an end in 1815, England's forests had been decimated to build the ships that helped to defeat Napoleon. The growth of the great industrial cities in early nineteenth-century England, and the expansion of the canal network, had also contributed to the loss of woodlands, for the wood was used as firewood and for building. Although wood was rapidly being replaced by coal for cooking and heating, and for industry, in areas distant from coalfields the ravages caused by felling were still evident in the mid-nineteenth century. Yet, by the end of the century, there was more woodland in the English countryside than there had been at the beginning.

Woods always had a role in the rural economy. In Berkshire, Miss Mitford and her semi-fictional companions loved to walk among the trees. But the woodland beauties could not stand for ever because of the commercial value of the bark and timber. They 'were approaching an open grove of magnificent oaks on the other side, when sounds other than of nightingales burst on our ear, the deep and frequent strokes of the woodman's axe, and emerging from the Pinge we discovered the havoc which that axe had committed. Above twenty of the finest trees lay stretched on the velvet turf. There they lay in every shape and form of devastation: some bare trunks stripped ready for the timber carriage, with the bark built up in long piles at the side; some with the spoilers busy about them, stripping, hacking, hewing; others with their noble branches, their brown and fragrant roots all fresh as if they were

Oak bark being cut and stacked, in a painting by David Bates. The bark would be dried in a rick before being crushed and sent to the tanner. He would make 'ooze' from the bark and water, and leave the hides to soak in it for a month to six weeks.

alive – majestic corpses, the slain of today! The grove was like a field of battle.' Even the birds, she felt, seemed to be singing a requiem for the fallen.

The wood bark was used for tanning leather, and women and children were set the task of stripping and stacking the outer sheaths of fallen trees, or of part-stripping the bark of standing trees, oak being the principal tree treated in this way. In general, the demand for home-grown hardwood was declining, especially after 1862, when the age of wooden naval ships came to a close. The trees planted in the wake of the Napoleonic Wars which had not yet come to maturity were to be left to stand.

Charcoal-burning was a trade that was carried on in some woodland areas, notably in the Lake District. As furnaces were no longer fired by charcoal, the product was destined mainly for domestic use and for artists' sketching materials. The last charcoal-fired iron-making furnace had closed down in 1828, in Sussex; the demise of charcoal-burning helped to preserve the wooded valleys of the Weald.

In much of England, clearing woods for farming was a process that was carried on until as late as the 1870s, with some of the ancient royal forests such as Hainault Forest in Essex or Delamere Forest in Cheshire being grubbed up with official approval. Then, in 1878, one of the first conservationist Acts of Parliament was passed, to preserve Epping Forest and to maintain it as a managed public open space. It was to be 'a lung to help London breathe', and from that success sprang the movement that gradually gained momentum to preserve the countryside.

Thereafter, the area of replanted woodland came to exceed that of the area cleared and, between 1870 and 1905, the extent of woodland in England grew by almost a quarter, to some 1,700,000 acres. Land where trees had once been was replanted with hazel, ash, sweet chestnut, oak and hornbeam, which were cropped at regular intervals, from five years to twenty. Coppiced timber was used for gates, fences, hurdles and hop-poles.

There were jobs not only in felling and barking the trees, and sawing the timber into planks, but also in the woodworking crafts of turning, joinery, cooperage and hurdle-making. Brushwood and fallen branches were collected as firewood for the cottage homes, and the child or older woman carrying home a bundle of faggots was a familiar part of the village scene.

Animals foraged in the woods, and country people searched for the edible fungi in autumn, when the nuts on the hazel, sweet chestnut and beech trees were ripening. Nut-gathering according to Miss Mitford was one of the most enjoyable village activities. Everyone would go out to gather the nuts which were 'in such abundance, that it seems as if there were not a boy in the parish, nor a young man, nor a young woman – for a basket of nuts is the universal tribute of country gallantry'.

Woodmen cutting timber; from these large-girthed trees came the raw material for buildings, ships and boats, wagons and railway sleepers.

This figure is working the underwood, smaller pieces from coppiced or pollarded trees, which might be used for fuel or any number of small wooden items: thatching spars, handles, pea and bean sticks, barrel hoops or implements.

THE SEA

ALL ALONG THE ENGLISH COAST are small seaside communities that were once thriving fishing villages. The tide and the mood of the sea governed the lives of the men and women who had made their homes in them as firmly as the farming calendar and the weather ruled the lives of country people: and, it was their livelihood.

Fishing villages were often isolated from other communities and were self-contained, having their own looks and traditions. In some, upturned boats were converted into sheds or even into small cottages, and the ordinary cottages, just as Tom Taylor evoked them, still smacked of the sea:

> . . . from roof or floor;
> As if some stranded hull to house had grown,
> And might up-anchor still, and float away.

The continuous round of making and repairing nets, baiting the pots and traps, caulking and cleaning boats, and setting out into the coastal waters in search of fish, was played out in villages that often huddled in little clefts in the coastal rocks or turned their faces away from the prevailing winds. Arthur Munby was amazed, on a visit to the Yorkshire coast in 1868, to encounter young women from the fishing villages who quite happily scaled the sheer cliffs to or from their otherwise inaccessible homes: 'I, the man of the party, was left in a ridiculous position; a useless spectator of these vigorous athletics.'

Clovelly, on the north coast of Cornwall, was a place apart, cut off by its unique topography from the outside. Charles Kingsley spent part of his boyhood there, 'crawling up the paved stairs inaccessible to cart or carriage'. It was a scene described by Charles Dickens in 1860 before the tourist trade had reached this most picturesque of all villages by the sea: 'From the sea-beach to the cliff top, the two irregular rows of white houses, placed opposite to one another, and twisting here and there, rose like the sides of a

Fishermen put to sea while children on the beach surround an old salt, enthralled by his stories; he sits with his pots for catching lobster and crab. A painting by John Henry Mole.

A life constrained by tide and weather. The fishermen in Thomas J. Lloyd's painting stand idle at the doorways of their whitewashed cottages. Nets dry on the sea wall and the boats are drawn up on the beach, left bare at low tide. The railways would speed the catches to the large towns, allowing fish to be introduced into the diet of many more people in Victorian England.

long succession of crooked ladders, and you climbed up the village by the staves between, some six feet wide or so, and made of sharp, irregular stones. The old pack saddle, long laid aside in most parts of England, flourished here intact... As the beasts of burden ascended laden, or descended light, they got so lost at intervals in the floating clouds of village smoke, that they seemed to dive down some of the village chimneys and come to the surface again far off.' The fishermen of this village, as elsewhere around the coast, depended on a good catch. The demands of London and the other great cities were felt everywhere.

Fishing became a considerably more organized industry in Victorian times, especially where the cheap and nutritious herring was concerned. As the herring season went on through the summer, and the shoals of the 'silver darlings' moved down through the North Sea, so village after village sprang into action. Women from the north of Scotland would follow the fish down the coast to Yorkshire and finally into Suffolk, working at gutting and salting the fish alongside the local women. In some places, notably on the coast of Northumberland where speedy access to wider markets was difficult, fishing villages developed a trade in curing and smoking the herring. Craster became famous as the source of the best kippers, while further down the east coast Great Yarmouth's speciality was bloaters, herrings smoked whole.

Work could be heavily seasonal, and from time to time fishermen and their families had to find other employment. Men from some of the Suffolk fishing villages, for example, would go across country to work in the breweries of Burton-on-Trent in the slack months of the year. In the fishing season, the lack of fish might spell disaster, and moreover the sea with its storms and rapidly changing moods could be a vicious opponent of the fisherman.

At Morwenstow, on the north Cornish coast near the Devon border, Robert Stephen Hawker, the eccentric vicar, became obsessed with the perils of the sea, risking his life to save men cast up on the rocks in shipwrecks or giving washed-up corpses a decent burial. Although they might suffer cruelly themselves if caught in a storm at sea, Hawker's parishioners treated a wreck off their treacherous coast as a providential gift for it could bring timber, a useful cargo, and perhaps the belongings of wealthy

The muscle of fishermen was needed to draw boats up on the shore, as in these sketches (left) by G. Chambers, for few fishing villages had the luxury of a purpose-built harbour. Tree trunks might serve as rollers on the most difficult beaches, and there were systems of winches.

passengers who had drowned. The Cornish child going to bed, it was said, prayed: 'God bless Father 'n' Mother an' zend a ship ta shore 'fore mornin'.'

In coastal villages, lifeboats and rescue services were set up. That at the picturesque Yorkshire fishing village of Robin Hood's Bay was established in 1881 after a disaster at sea during a tremendous storm. The Whitby lifeboat was called out and had to be hauled over the snow-bound hills to reach the bay, which took so long that many lives were lost.

There was another side to these fishing villages, too, for many of them gradually became tourist and holiday places for the well-to-do and the town dweller. The Victorians invented the seaside holiday, building on the sea bathing that the later Georgians had pioneered at resorts such as Weymouth and Brighton. In 1847, Queen Victoria went into the sea on the Isle of Wight for the first time. 'I thought it was delightful till I put my head under the water,' she wrote, 'when I thought I should be stifled.' Francis Kilvert went to seaside villages for his annual holiday in the 1870s, using bathing machines or swimming from the beach as the local custom demanded – and being angered by the new insistence that he should wear bathing drawers to cover his nakedness.

Many fishermen, like this south-coast man with his fresh plaice, sold the fish they caught directly from the beach or from their boats. Watercolour by William Collins.

CHAPTER 5

ON THE ROAD

THE ROAD AND RAILWAY

'EVERY TRAVELLER IN HAMPSHIRE remembers the road that sways with airy motion and bird-like curves down from the high land of clay and flint through the chalk to the sand and the river. It doubles round the head of a coombe, and the whole descent is through beech woods uninterrupted and all but impenetrable to the eye. . . It is said to have been made more than half a century ago to take the place of the rash straight coach-road which now enters near its base.' Travel by road in Victorian England was a vastly improved affair compared with what it had been before, as Edward Thomas recognized; and yet roads retained an old magic.

Long-distance road travel through the countryside first became easy with the stage and mail coaches, from the late eighteenth century. George Eliot described how, on the mail coach, 'the traveller passed rapidly from one phase of English life to another: after looking down on a village dingy with coal-dust, noisy with the shaking of looms, he might skirt a parish all of fields, high hedges, and deep-rutted lanes', and so come to appreciate the quickening pace of change in the Victorian countryside.

The network of stage coach services was probably at its most extensive when Queen Victoria came to the throne, linking all the main towns. Smaller towns, villages and hamlets that were on the coach routes, benefited considerably, though they suffered from the dust that the traffic brought; other villages needed the services of the local carrier's cart to ferry people and goods to the nearest staging post.

Stone-breaking, essential to the maintenance of the road surfaces in countryside and town, was to the Victorians a symbol of poverty and degradation. It was a task allotted to old men, or one that vagrants were obliged to perform in return for a night's shelter in the workhouse. Like every country task, it needed skill. In

G. W. Mote's painting of stone-breakers in 1868. Stone-breaking was one of the hardest of rural tasks. Working beside the roads meant that the stone-breaker learnt all the news from passers-by, and a traditional reply to a question was 'Ask the stone-breaker'.

A covered cart stops at a toll gate on a turnpike road. The charge depended on the number of people and animals and the size of the vehicle.

his Norfolk village, Rider Haggard made an attempt at breaking the tough granite blocks, 'and a poor hand I made of the task'.

The variety of the wheeled traffic in the countryside increased rapidly in the course of the nineteenth century: there were many different forms of carriage, gigs, spring carts, governess carts, the pony and trap. In the course of one year, Francis Kilvert travelled in a brougham, an open-topped carriage, a mail phaeton, a dog cart and a fly. He also walked a great deal. And he used the railway.

A traveller observed in the 1850s, when railway mania gripped England and the rail network was expanding rapidly, that 'had the double tailed comet passed that way, the country people could scarcely have been more interested by the spectacle... The men at work in the fields and quarries stood like statues... and women in their best gowns and bonnets fled from the villages and congregated at the corner of every intersecting lane... Every horse was on the alert, viewing the huge moving body as it approached with a mixture of fear and surprise.'

By the end of Queen Victoria's reign, the railways were familiar to everybody, and they stretched into the remotest corners of the land – Hartland, tucked away on the north Devon coast, claimed the distinction for itself of being the English parish 'farthest from railways'. Landowners who held out against the railway passing through their lands found themselves bypassed; some held aloof, while others then scrambled to join in. The two grand stations just outside Bakewell in Derbyshire, only a mile apart, were built for the Dukes of Devonshire and Rutland, who had put every obstacle in the way of the railway builders and then found they wanted an appropriately self-important station each.

Many country people were unable to afford the railway fares, except as a special treat, but the trains brought townspeople into much easier and more regular contact with rural England. While travelling, in Robert Louis Stevenson's words:

> All of the sights of the hill and the plain
> Fly as thick as driving rain;
> And ever again, in the wink of an eye
> Painted stations whistle by.

Country produce was increasingly sent by rail, and town demand for milk helped to save English agriculture from ruin in the 1880s.

During the course of the nineteenth century tolls on roads, bridges, harbours and causeways gradually disappeared.

A train steams through the Hertfordshire countryside at Berkhamsted, an engraving for the 1840 edition of the London and Birmingham Railway Guide.

The milk train ruled the life of Alison Uttley's farmhouse family. Even on Christmas Day, 'the churns were silently rolled through thick snow, and lifted on the cart... Susan made the milk tickets, Becky polished the lamp, and Dan drank a brimming mug of tea, and hurried out into the cold night, down the steep snowy hill' to the railway halt.

In Richard Jefferies' Wiltshire, 'Each tin bears a brazen badge engraved with the name of the milkman who will retail its contents in distant London. It may be delivered to the countess in Belgravia, and reach her dainty lip in the morning chocolate, or it may be eagerly swallowed up by the half-starved children of some back court in the purlieus of Seven Dials.' Sometimes dozens of different farmers' carts would converge on the station or the wayside halt, each bringing a churn or two that would be loaded on to the train, and empty cans carried back for the next day. By 1880, twenty million gallons of milk a year were being brought into London by rail – three times the amount of fifteen years before. The main line of the Great Western Railway through Berkshire and Wiltshire became known as the 'Milky Way'.

Elsenham Station on the Cambridge/Ely line, opened in 1845.

The station at Alton Towers, the seat of the Earl of Shrewsbury, on the North Staffordshire railway; in 1886. Although many landowners fiercely resisted lines running through their estates, once constructed they often demanded stations for their exclusive use and built in the architectural style of their choice.

VILLAGE INNS

The squire sits quietly reading the newspaper in the village public house, a tankard at his elbow, in the painting by William Mulready. The inn was where the newspapers were often to be found.

I N Victorian villages it was customary to find a great many drinking places. Some were the alehouses of former times, small and frequently disreputable cottages licensed (or, as often as not, unlicensed) to brew and sell beer. Others were the larger public houses, sometimes built as such and with more rooms and amenities. There working men and smaller farmers spent many a happy evening. Largest and most important of all were the roadside inns, which were usually staging posts for the old mail and stage coaches. They were a common sight along the main through roads, with their sweeping entrances, or in the middle of villages. These inns offered accommodation and stabling, and perhaps fresh horses for the travellers.

In Thomas Hood's poem about 'Our Village' there were fifty-five dwellings, and 'plenty of public houses – two Foxes, one Green Man, three Bunch of Grapes, one Crown, and six King's Heads'. Of these, the Green Man was reckoned to be the best because it could put together for hire some semblance of a horse and carriage. In real-life Wortham in 1860, the Reverend Richard Cobbold noted five drinking establishments. Two, the Queen's Head and the Magpie, were inns, roadside establishments which had seen happier days when the coaching trade was busier before the coming of the railways.

For the most part, the drinking dens were similar in appearance to ordinary domestic interiors. Tables and stools were set around the room with the publican or alehouse-keeper serving beer from a jug drawn at barrels in an adjacent room. In the inn which Tess's parents frequented in Thomas Hardy's *Tess of the D'Urbervilles*, customers were served in the landlady's bedroom, since she was not licensed to sell beer on the premises.

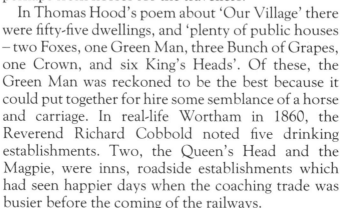

Joe Fry's Inn, painted by Anson Martin. The horses on the Doncaster stage coach are being changed by the ostlers, while passengers alight in search of sustenance; meanwhile, the Royal Mail speeds on its way. After their early Victorian heyday, the coaching inns were superseded by the railway.

The Crossed Guns.

The Swan.

The Ship.

The Bell.

Outdoor games and skittle alleys attracted customers, while pub games such as shove ha'penny or some local form of indoor bowls drew people in on cold nights. Traditionally, some of these games were played for money, though sometimes for beer, but by the 1880s gaming legislation had made the placing of wagers on pub games illegal. Richard Jefferies was one who bitterly regretted the change: 'Why deprive the man who labours all day in wet and storm of so simple a pleasure in the evening? Now that he is practically deprived of his skittles and other such games, he has no amusement left except drink.'

Flora Thompson described the public house in her native Juniper Hill as 'its own social centre': 'There the adult population gathered every evening, to sip its half-pints, drop by drop, to make them last, and to discuss local events, wrangle over politics or farming methods, or to sing a few songs... It was exclusively a men's gathering. Their wives never accompanied them; though sometimes a woman who had got her family off hand, and so had a few halfpence to spend on herself, would knock at the back door with a bottle or jug and perhaps linger a little, herself unseen, to listen to what was going on within.' Jefferies went further, and called the alehouse the labourer's 'stock exchange, his reading room, his club and his assembly rooms'.

Some public houses and alehouses had been designated stopping-places on the routes of tramping artisans and cattle drovers, places where they would expect to be helped on their way and which extended a particular welcome to members of a craft. The many Masons' Arms and Square and Compasses around the countryside were originally 'houses of call' for itinerant workers, while many a bleak upland place still has a Drovers' Arms to mark the route along which herds of cattle passed.

Many publicans had other part-time occupations, as barbers or carriers perhaps, or as small shopkeepers. Children in Flora Thompson's home village used to knock at the back door of the Wagon and Horses to buy candles or treacle or cheese, and eavesdrop on their parents and neighbours. From the records of the courts, it seems that many publicans were also involved in less law-abiding activities, receiving stolen goods or protecting poachers from the law. Public houses were the centres of agitation and dissent in the outbreaks of rural violence that characterized

The Magpie and Stump.

The Goat.

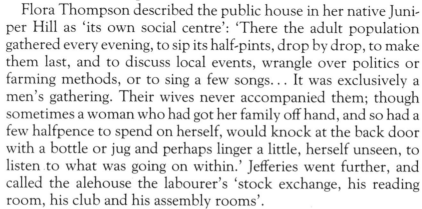

The White Horse.

The Sun.

Characteristic sign boards for pubs and inns (opposite), an iconography dating from past centuries. Many had their origins in heraldry, such as the Swan, and the Magpie and Stump seen here.

the 1830s and 1840s, when farm workers made clear their many grievances by burning down farm buildings and hay ricks. Drinking places had long been known, in a phrase belonging to earlier centuries, as 'nurseries of naughtiness'.

The growth in agricultural trade unionism in the 1870s, which continued on in some country areas such as Norfolk until the First World War, was not so often centred on the public houses as earlier disaffection had been. The driving force behind unionization in many areas was the Chapel, and especially Primitive Methodism, which set its face against the 'demon drink'. The temperance movement in late Victorian Britain eventually made its way into the country, where children were corralled into signing the pledge in their infant scrawl.

Some commentators noted – usually, like Hardy, with ill-disguised distaste – that public houses had occasionally been transformed into temperance coffee houses. Where pubs remained in wicked evidence, restrictions were increasingly placed on their activities: fewer licences were issued in many country areas in the later nineteenth century, and opening hours were shortened. Jefferies recorded: that 'Since the earlier closing, the village streets have been comparatively free from drunken men.' He quickly tempered that with the remark that, 'The agricultural labourer is the most lamb-like of drunkards.'

The interior of a typical village inn, with the settle sheltering the backs of the drinkers from cold draughts and the fireplace providing welcome warmth.

ITINERANT TRADERS

WANDERING MEN AND, LESS FREQUENTLY, WOMEN were often to be seen along the roads and lanes of the Victorian countryside, selling their wares, performing small services, mending broken objects or providing entertainment, as they passed through. William Brighty Rands's lines seem to sum up the magic felt by the Victorians to surround a trader on the roads:

> I wish I lived in a caravan,
> With a horse to drive, like the pedlar-man!
> Where he comes from, nobody knows,
> Or where he goes to, but on he goes!

The general pedlar, or packman, was the longest established of these, buying his goods from fairs or town shops and selling from

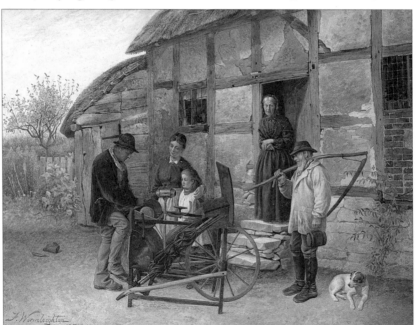

The knifegrinder, a painting of 1875 by Francis Wormleighton. The knifegrinder travelled the countryside pushing his grindstone on a cart. Here, a farm labourer waits with his scythe while cottagers are having their kitchen knives sharpened.

Children gather round the toysellers on the village green, in a painting by James Stokeld of 1864. Furious eyes are fixed on the spoilt girl who cannot make up her mind. Toys and other small goods manufactured in the towns only found their way into rural areas with pedlars, or else they were bought and brought home from markets and fairs.

his pack as he went. He might have cloth to sell, needles and pins and thread. Frequently he carried cheap brooches, handkerchiefs or little toys, among them the pedlar dolls that were a miniature, though often female, version of himself. Where settlement was scattered and access difficult, pedlars were the main suppliers of many common household goods. In the Gloucestershire hills behind Stroud, distribution was largely by donkey as pedlars delivered and hawked around fresh produce, cloth and newspapers, and the area acquired the local name 'Neddyshire'.

An itinerant knifegrinder. As an observer wrote, 'there is a picturesque diversity in the various machines travelling about the country; some of these are transported all over England by knifegrinders who carry them on their backs, others are fitted up with a small cart with a forge. These people frequently unite the brazier with the cutler.'

As the pedlar opened his pack at a cottage door, he opened a window on to a larger world of goods to buy. He also helped to open minds to a wider world through printed material, since he carried books and ballad sheets as part of his stock and, later on, newspapers. There would be a ready market for his flimsy, cheaply printed books – twopence coloured, penny plain.

The ballads that were hawked around were the tabloid newspapers of the day, written in London and distributed through the provinces, telling of events great and small – battles, horrible murders, rural discontent. The almanacs with their predictions as flimsy as the paper on which they were printed had been a stock item in pedlars' packs since at least the mid-seventeenth century.

Sometimes hawkers carried the most surprising things. In 1898 Rider Haggard met a pedlar on the road from whom he bought a piece of church silver – a paten, and probably sixteenth-century. This was not the first time they had met: 'From this pedlar I have from time to time purchased some of the best things in my small collection, notably a little bronze, which I believe to be one of the very few extant portraits of the great Egyptian queen, Taia!'

By that time, though, pedlars were considerably less common; they had been superseded by village shops and the local carriers who dealt with the shops in towns on behalf of their customers. Only one packman came to Flora Thompson's home village in the

1880s: 'He would turn aside from the turnpike and come plodding down the narrow hamlet road, an old white-headed, white-bearded man, still hale and rosy, although almost bent double under the heavy, black canvas-covered pack he carried strapped on his shoulders. "Anything out of the pack today?" he would ask at each house, and, at the least encouragement, fling down his load and open it on the doorstep. He carried a tempting variety of goods: dress-lengths and shirt-lengths and remnants to make up for the children; aprons and pinafores, plain and fancy; corduroys for the men, and coloured scarves and ribbons for Sunday wear.'

Where packmen were found, they were often working for drapers in the larger towns, rather than being the independent men of the highway they had once been. But they were far from being the only itinerant traders on the country roads. The pages of Thomas Hardy's Wessex novels describe several others: the reddle-man, selling dye and red from top to toe, is one of the central characters in *The Return of the Native*; and in parts of the west of England – and as described in *The Woodlanders* – the itinerant cider-maker made a seasonal appearance: 'He looked and smelt like Autumn's very brother, his face being sunburnt to wheat-colour, his eyes blue as corn-flowers, his sleeves and leggings dyed with fruit stains, his hands clammy with the sweet juice of apples, his hat sprinkled with pips, and everywhere about him that atmosphere of cider which at its first return each season has such an indescribable fascination for those who have been born and bred among the orchards.'

George Chambers' watercolour sketch of an itinerant family cooking a meal. They would have had little choice but to sleep in tents or, more rarely, caravans, as they plied their trade on the road.

Flora Thompson's grandfather in rural Oxfordshire had been an eggler, 'buying up eggs from farms and cottages and selling them at markets and shopkeepers' – a particular type of higgler or middleman. Richard Jefferies described characters such as the china-seller, who would set up at the roadside with crockery and tinware, in front of 'a backcloth painted with icebergs and penguins and polar bears'. Along with him in rural Wiltshire and Berkshire in the later years of the century were many representatives of town businesses taking their trade out into the country-side, where getting to town or to market proved difficult: 'The rural butcher has his round, his cart tail being counter and chopping block, sometimes taking back eggs and farm produce to sell at his shop; the grocer whose cart is covered with advertisements and hung with household requisites; the oilman who has a carefully mapped route for every day in the week; the leather seller who supplies the cobbler and those who mend their own boots.'

There were many other itinerants who performed useful services. The chairmender was welcomed in many areas, repairing the worn-out seats of chairs that had seen better days. The old chairmender, in Tom Taylor's version, was a tent-dweller, who stayed in the neighbourhood for only a day or two:

> You'd say I had no more call to chairs
> Than yon cow to a steeple.

But he was adept at his craft, at plaiting the rush and cane:

> The chairs I mend will see to end
> More than one set o' sitters.

The travelling tinsmith or tinker likewise mended worn-out household items, those pots and pans that had been burned or worn through, by patching or re-lining them. Cottage gardens were often supplied by seedmen. John Chamberlain, from Huntingdonshire, travelled round in the 1860s going into public houses to hawk his goods, with his patter: 'Any gentleman want any carrot seeds, onion seeds, parsnip seeds, lettuce seeds, parsley seeds, radish seeds, or any Windsor fine peas? What I can't get today I'll bring another day.'

Fresh produce was also hawked around the villages at certain times of the year. The cherry-seller or apple-seller would bring round baskets of ripe fruit to sell, crying their wares along the lanes and village streets. In market garden areas like the Vale of Evesham, asparagus might be sold by travelling men; girls in southern counties sold bunches of watercress; and in areas near the coast women from the fishing villages came inland with their baskets of freshly landed fish. The classic Frenchman with his strings of onions for sale made his first appearance in the late Victorian years.

There were those who sold, and those who entertained. An organ-grinder, perhaps an exotic-seeming Italian, might travel the country roads with a mischievous monkey to pass the hat round. C.S. Calverley wrote lines on hearing the travelling barrel-organ:

A travelling puppet show, painted by J. L. Lucas. Travelling entertainers appeared in the villages from time to time, but especially for local fairs and feast days. Punch and Judy were favourite puppet characters, and children delighted in Punch's outrageous exploits, which included flinging the bodies of the murdered Judy and their child into the street.

131

Dearly do I love thy grinding;
Joy to meet thee on thy road
Where thou prowlest through the blinding
Dust with that stupendous load

and he thought that tough men who heard the organ were made 'kinder to their bullocks and their wives'.

Travelling showmen might bring a dancing bear that would shamble through its routine to the delight and fright of village children. Sometimes these itinerant entertainers came on their own, but they might otherwise travel as part of a larger fairground troupe; at the end of the nineteenth century they might also have a set of steam-driven rides to entertain children on the village green. Even if they did not stop, they provided a thrilling spectacle, especially when in the early years of the new century a great steam engine for powering the rides led the procession.

Travelling actors were less common than they had once been, but occasionally a group might pass through and put on a show in a convenient barn or the yard of a village inn. Peripatetic entertainers in later years brought a magic lantern show to villages, precursors of the travelling cinema of the silent film era, and opened up a new world of experience. The show groups were usually travelling from one fun fair to another, and had stopped on their way to entertain a village.

Also trudging the highways and byways were the tramps and vagrants. Tramping had been a recognized way for working men to find work by travelling round until the early decades of the nineteenth century, either as new members of a trade finding their feet or because of a lack of work in their home area. They used the alehouses, established houses of call, on their route as places to stay while seeking work. That system was well in decline by the mid-nineteenth century; but the number of tramps in a more modern sense, vagrants to the Victorians, increased substantially. The

The hawker travelled the countryside on a horse or a donkey with his stock of novelties, ribbons, threads, haberdashery, matches and even song-sheets.

gentlemen of the road, usually single men, had their own ways, signalling to one another as to whether or not they might be welcomed in a particular house or village. The workhouses were obliged to provide overnight accommodation and a small amount of food, usually bread and water, for vagrants who were completely penniless; in return, vagrants usually performed some menial work, such as stone-breaking, but at least the workhouse offered shelter and a bed, however hard.

In the bitter aftermath of the Irish famine in the 1840s, many destitute Irish families came to England, travelling and begging. Some were barely distinguishable from the gypsies with whom they increasingly became confused, others maintained a proud aloofness. When 'three girls tall dressed in ragged black with naked legs and feet' went begging through Francis Kilvert's village one July day, the sight was arresting. Kilvert, like most Victorian villagers, seems not to have given them anything; there were often so many vagrants that giving, once started, would never seem to stop. In the wake of the hard times in agriculture in the 1880s, there was a further increase in vagrancy, as men, and sometimes also their families, laid off from the land wandered in search of help and shelter. The fear of vagrants and beggars, and the hostility they often encountered, meant that they often caught the attention of the police, who arrested and occasionally briefly imprisoned them before sending them out of the district.

Whatever the difficulties in which some of those wandering the roads found themselves, the Victorian memories of itinerants are mainly in the nature of those recaptured by William Brighty Rands, of the picturesque travelling pedlar and entertainer:

> His caravan has windows two,
> And a chimney of tin, that the smoke comes through;
> He has a wife, with a baby brown,
> And they go riding from town to town.

The pedlar went from place to place on foot. Both pedlars and hawkers had to produce certificates of good character and buy a licence to sell their wares.

GYPSIES

'THE PICTURE OF the Rural Life of England must be wholly defective which should omit those singular and most picturesque squatters on heaths and in lanes – the Gipsies,' wrote William Howitt. 'They make part and parcel of the landscape scenery.' Their dark skins and flashing eyes, their strange language, their brightly painted caravans, and their restless way of life, all made them seem exotic. Running away with the 'raggle-taggle gypsies' was the exciting theme of many songs and stories.

Romany and romance went hand in hand. Howitt had come across fashionable town girls in the woods of Surrey who were dressing themselves up as gypsies and acting out the romantic charm of the woodland life. Theodore Watts-Dunton's novel *Aylwin* was one of the many colourful Victorian books and poems written to celebrate the gypsy way of life, and Watts-Dunton went so far as to write that: 'In Great Britain it is the Gipsies alone who understand nature's supreme charm, and enjoy her largesse as it used to be enjoyed. . . before the Children of the Roof invaded the Children of the Open Air. . .'

Best-known of all was George Borrow's *Lavengro*. Borrow himself had been a 'Romany rye', having lived with the gypsies; and the romance of their lives – the travelling, the tents, the horse-dealing, the snake in a basket, the fortune-telling, the fist-fights, the sixth senses – found expression in his book.

For the gamekeeper, however, the gypsies presented a very different aspect: 'they are adepts at poaching, and each van is usually accompanied by a couple of dogs. The movements of these people are so irregular that it is impossible always to be ready for them.' There seemed to be 'no end to the tricks and subterfuges practised' by the travellers. In some counties, the new rural police forces of the 1850s and 1860s used to move on gypsies, and other vagrants, with a considerable show of force. Across the country, from Shropshire to Kent, gaggles of travelling people were always the first on whom to pin all the blame for petty thefts and poaching, even though the evidence often pointed in quite the contrary direction.

William Shayer's 'A Gypsy Encampment in the New Forest' contains all the romantic elements of gypsy life that appealed to the Victorians: a covered cart, donkeys and ponies, and curs.

The gypsies, as well as being romantic, were feared for their rootlessness and different looks and behaviour. 'Gypsy blood' was a term common in many villages to explain, or condone, a ne'er-do-well; and certain characteristics in a villager might only be explained away by gypsy blood. The people of Blaxhall, Suffolk, remembered an old lady called Black Mary in the 1880s: 'Her hair was black as a raven's right up to her death. But, they say, she knew the gypsy's hair patent as she was herself descended from a travelling woman. The lotion was made from the grease of a hedgehog, soot from the chimney, a drop of eau de cologne or lavender water to make it smell sweet and a few drops of olive oil. She used it regularly, and even when she was an old woman her hair grew down to her waist and there wasn't a grey strand in it.'

The gypsy families, as they travelled in their caravans, tended to keep to the same circuits each year, so villagers knew when to expect these colourful creatures to pass – and to fear or cheer their arrival. Many rural localities have a Gypsy Lane, where travelling families established a winter camp, and sometimes acquired an informal property title to the waste land where they regularly halted their caravans. The Gypsy Lane at Cowley, just outside Oxford, was so named in the 1861 Census: it was where the enumerator took down the details of all the gypsy families – or as much detail as the gypsies were prepared to tell the gorgio.

'Sometimes,' wrote Miss Mitford, 'we used to see a gypsy procession passing along the common, like an eastern caravan, men, women, and children, donkeys and dogs.' She was rather startled to encounter such 'Spanish-looking' men on one of her solitary walks.

Several gypsy families camped semi-permanently in the margins of the New Forest and on the heaths of Surrey. These empty areas of scrubland were ideal for the gypsies, for they found there wood for the clothes pegs, skewers and little boxes they made to sell, spring flowers to hawk around the towns and villages, rabbits for their dogs and especially their greyhounds to catch, brushwood and furze for their fires and rough grazing for their horses.

The gypsies were horse-dealers in many country areas, providing the little working ponies that helped many small farmers and traders to get by. Some did a more organized trade, buying horses in Wales and the north-west, and bringing them south and east. Appleby Horse Fair is the last vestige of that way of life.

The Victorians remarked that the gypsy men kept aloof from ordinary villagers unless they had particular business to do, while the women and children were always approaching people in the lanes or coming to the cottage doors, selling their pegs or their nosegays, and telling fortunes. They possessed powers of foresight and curses that set them apart from the local people. Flora Thompson, working at the post office in Fringford, sometimes wrote letters for the gypsies. Photographs taken at the end of the last century show the main way in which gypsy children differed from others. Most children at that time would wear white aprons or pinafores – of a whiteness that must have been difficult to maintain – and they would wear hats too; gypsy children and their mothers usually wore neither.

Again of the gypsies, Miss Mitford wrote, 'There is nothing under the sun that harmonizes so well with nature, especially in her woodland recesses, as that picturesque people, who are, so to say, the wild genus – the pheasants and roebucks of the human race.'

CHAPTER 6

MARKETS AND MERRYMAKING

MARKETS AND FAIRS

E VERY ENGLISH VILLAGE WAS within reach of a town and its market. Often there were a number of small market towns dotted around, and each had a different day in the week for its market. Most of the markets were of ancient foundation, and for centuries on a Wednesday, a Saturday or whichever was the appointed day, country people had brought their produce to town, to sell in the market place from a stall or from the steps of the market cross. There they spent the money they earned or had saved up on things they needed for the house, the garden or the farm. As the old rhyme had it:

To market, to market
To buy a fat pig.
Home again, home again,
Jiggety-jig.

Market towns supported a far wider range of shops and craftsmen than any village could be expected to do, and they offered the services of the professional men needed by country people from time to time: the doctor, the surgeon, the apothecary, the solicitor. Some towns had the importance of being county towns, or cathedral towns. In that case, as with Anthony Trollope's Barchester, there was a considerable veneer of gentility to the ordinary functioning of market and trade.

On market day there was the constant flow into town of wheeled vehicles from the villages: farm carts, wagons, gigs, and grander carriages. All, as Richard Jefferies described it, was bustle: 'Cart-horses furbished up for sale, with strawbound tails and glistening skins; baaing flocks of sheep; squeaking pigs; bullocks with their heads held ominously low...; lads rushing hither and thither; dogs barking; everything and everybody crushing,

'Off to Market', a painting by William Mulready. The cart is ready to be loaded high and precariously with live chickens and baskets of vegetables for the slow journey into town.

Sheep and cattle throng the market place and the streets in St Albans on a busy market day in the painting by Henry Milbourne. Country people made their way by cart and by foot to the town, where all manner of bargains were struck. In the evening sheep and cattle were driven home by their new owners.

jostling, pushing through the narrow street.' And the elderly shepherd on his day off, with a few pence in his pocket, made his way toward the beer-house.

No village operated on its own, for each was part of a network of trade that centred on a local town, and village people went there and back. In Thomas Hardy's Caster-bridge, the needs of the surrounding area were reflected in the goods sold in its shops: 'Scythes, reap-hooks, sheep-shears, bill-hooks, spades, mattocks, and hoes at the ironmonger's; beehives, butter firkins, churns, milking stools and pails, hay-rakes, field flagons, and seed-lips at the cooper's; cart-ropes and plough harness at the saddler's; carts, wheelbarrows, and mill gear at the wheelwright's and machinist's; horse embrocations at the chemist's; at the glover's and leather-cutter's, hedging gloves, thatcher's knee-caps, ploughman's leg-gings, villagers' pattens and clogs.' The taverns normally did their best trade on market day. In some of the smaller towns, the place only came alive once a week, to return to slumber until the next market day.

In addition to the ordinary market trade, there were some market towns – and especially the larger ones – that specialized in a particular type of farm produce or animal. Cattle markets and sheep markets had weekly or monthly sales, where farmers and meat or livestock traders bargained with each other or, increas-ingly in the Victorian period, an auctioneer solicited bids in the auction ring. Butter or cheese were the special feature of markets in certain areas, or one market in a locality might do a particular trade in them.

A prominent Victorian feature in many a market town today is the corn exchange, usually a grand public building decorated with statues of Ceres or some other symbol of the harvest. Grain mar-keting expanded enormously in the nineteenth century; and whereas farmers had once brought their grain in sacks to sell to merchants or millers in the open market place, the growing prac-

William Howitt wrote, 'There are few things which give one such a feeling of the prosperity of the country as seeing the country people pour into a large town on market day... boys and girls... with baskets of tame rabbits, and bunches of cowslips, primroses and all kinds of flowers and country productions imaginable.'

A vignette of countryfolk at the close of market day. Howitt remarked: 'The farmers go riding and driving out three times as fast as they came in, for they are primed with good dinners and strong beer.'

tice was to bring a sample of wheat or barley to show the quality of what they had grown, a bargain being struck on the floor of a specially-constructed corn exchange. Dressed in their best, the farmers haggled with the corn traders who were supplying the needs of London and the growing industrial regions. It was on to such a trading floor that Bathsheba Everdene strode in Hardy's *Far from the Madding Crowd*, a lone woman amongst all the men, 'conscious of having broken into that dignified stronghold at last'.

One consequence of the greater commercialization of agriculture in the nineteenth century, and the difference caused by whether or not the railway passed through and trains stopped there, was that many smaller market towns declined, while a few larger centres prospered considerably at their expense. That was part of a long-term process, for many of the villages had an old market cross to show that markets had once upon a time been held in even so small a place.

As the regular weekly markets changed, so did the fairs which were such important events in the calendar of a country area. A. E. Housman's Shropshire lad was attracted to the annual delights of the fair:

The lads in their hundreds to Ludlow come in for the fair,
There's men from the barn and the forge and the mill and the fold,

The Old Market House in Pembridge, Herefordshire, drawn at the close of the Victorian era by S. R. Jones.

The lads for the girls and the lads for the liquor are there,
And there with the rest are the lads that will never be old.

The annual hiring of servants often took place at a fair – a 'statute fair' – in or near a town. Depending on the locality, it might be held around Michaelmas at the beginning of October, at Martinmas in early November, Lady Day in late March, or May Day. Francis Kilvert wrote in his diary of 'the great May Hiring Fair at Hay, and squadrons of horse came charging and battalions of foot tramping along the dusty roads to the town, more boys and fewer girls than usual. All day long the village has been very quiet, empty, most of the village folk being away at the fair. Now at 8 pm the roads are thronged with people pouring home again.'

The annual statute fair, as painted by J. Faed, was where men and women offered themselves for hire. Carters wore a piece of whipcord in their hats, shepherds a tuft of wool, servant-girls held a pail, a broom or a mop: hence it was also known as a 'mop fair'.

The hiring fair was a great day out, when the country roads would be busy the day long, and the streets of the town filled with fair-goers, some enjoying the sights, others striking a new bargain for the coming year. One man described the procedure as he had experienced it in Yorkshire at the turn of the century, an experience common to many previous generations: 'We would stand about in groups. . . until a farmer came along. After eyeing us over like so many oxen, he would say, "Nah, my lads, any on yer seeking a place?" Being warmed up with good ale, we answered truculently, or offhandedly at least, that we "didn't care a damn whether we got a place or not", and "What sort of chap are yer wanting?" ' He would then say and, after singling out a man or boy that took his fancy, would begin questioning him on his qualifications. In some parts of the country, servants and other workers looking to be hired would stand with the badge of their skill: a mop for a servant girl (hence the term 'mop fair'), a field tool or a horsewhip for a man. After the hiring was done and the new worker had received a token payment to secure the contract, the beer flowed; and the lump sum earned in the past year would be spent on the sideshows or stalls at the fair or in the shops. Young workers used the fairs as a good opportunity for match-making, and many a happy marriage had its origin in a meeting at the statute fair.

There were also the great trading fairs. Some were of a special nature, like the annual Sheep Fair in the centre of Boston, Lincolnshire. They were on a much grander scale than the weekly

markets and they attracted stallholders and pedlars from all around. But the main function of these ancient fairs was declining in Victorian England, in the face of competition from regular markets and the shops that were springing up in villages as well as in the towns. People no longer needed to stock up with goods such as cloth or sugar once or twice a year. They were turning into fun fairs, like the Goose Fair at Nottingham, or the Michaelmas Fair that still fills the main streets of Abingdon. With that transformation in the character of fairs went the added possibility of immorality and drinking, those twin scourges of Victorian respectability. A number of fairs were closed down by the authorities on the grounds that they had lost their trading character and had descended into licentiousness and drunkenness. Bury Fair, once one of the greatest of all English fairs, in the Suffolk town of Bury St Edmunds, which had attracted trade from across Europe and had been one of the high

As the nineteenth century progressed, fairs became not so much places to trade as events of entertainment; here a one-man, handbell band is accompanied by an entertainer in harlequin costume playing the salt-box.

points of the social calendar in the east of England, was closed down by the Home Secretary in 1857 amidst allegations of impropriety and regular drunken behaviour.

Most of the pleasures of the fair remained innocent, however. Some of the characters in Hardy's *The Mayor of Casterbridge* went to the fair field, which was based on that at Weyhill in Hampshire, 'which showed standing places and pens where many hundreds of horses and sheep had been exhibited and sold in the fore-noon, but were now in great part taken away... Yet the crowd was denser now than during the morning hours, the frivolous contingent of visitors included journeymen out for a holiday, a stray soldier or two home on furlough, village shopkeepers and the like... among the peep-shows, toy-stands, waxworks, inspired monsters, disinterested medical men who travelled for the public good, thimble-riggers, nick-nack vendors, and readers of Fate.' Mechanical rides added to all the fun of the fair.

An early form of roundabout or whirlygig. As the artist described it, 'the proprietor charges a halfpenny for each passenger while miserable straggling boys receive a few halfpennies for pushing it swiftly round.' Later in the century elaborately carved and glittering steam-powered merry-go-rounds would replace these simple affairs.

SPORTS AND GAMES

Village cricket, painted by John Ritchie. Cricket, played on an open green, emerged during the nineteenth century as the most popular of the summer village games, taking the place of regional ones such as the Kentish bat and trap and the knur and spell of the north-east.

IN MANY PARTS OF ENGLAND, cricket was the most popular village game. Shared by gentlemen and country people alike, it was played at the public schools and the universities, in country-house parks and on village greens. In the nineteenth century, important changes were introduced: round-arm bowling was sanctioned in 1835; county championships were founded; boundary lines were drawn for the first time; and individual cricketers became national heroes. Every village boy was to hear of W. G. Grace, whose batsmanship had transformed the game by the 1870s.

Victorian villagers, such as William Clift of Bramley, Hampshire, a farmer, recalled a cricket club being formed for the local landowner's son: 'we were all asked to join'. Refusals would not have been accepted. The amateur, the local man, was the backbone of village cricket.

Miss Mitford lauded the 'real solid, old-fashioned match between neighbouring parishes, where each attacks the other for honour and a supper, glory and half a crown a man. If there be any gentlemen amongst them, it is well – if not, it is so much the better.' She provided one of the classic nineteenth-century accounts of a village match, rehearsing all the players' virtues, and then the excitement of the game: 'These challengers – the famous eleven – how many did they get? Think! imagine! guess! – You cannot? – Well! they got twenty-two, or rather they got twenty; for two of theirs were short notches, and would never have been allowed, only that, seeing what they were made of, we and our umpires were not particular... Well, we went in. And what were our innings? Guess again! – guess! A hundred and sixty-nine! in spite of soaking showers, and wretched ground where the ball would not run a yard...

'And so we parted; the players retired to their supper, and we to our homes; all wet through, all good-humoured, and all happy – except the losers.'

Annual football matches without limitations on numbers were played in some villages, especially in the Midlands; the Shrove Tuesday football match in Ashbourne, Derbyshire, is still played – with no boundary.

Even a hamlet had its representative fighting man – often more than one – who visited the neighbouring villages on feast days, when there was a good deal of liquor flowing, boasting of his prowess to the local champions. Villagers such as 'the Okebourne and Clipstone men thwacked and banged each others' broad chests in true antique style', according to Jefferies.

Some of the adult games played in Victorian villages were the result of conscious revival, rather than survival from an earlier age. Quintain, a form of jousting against flour bags rather than knights in armour, was given a popularity in the nineteenth century by the gentry, as described by Anthony Trollope in *Barchester Towers*: ' "Here goes then," said Harry as he wheeled his horse round to get the necessary momentum of a sharp gallop. The quintain post stood right before him, and the square board at which he was to tilt was fairly in his way. If he hit that duly in the middle, and maintained his pace as he did so, it was calculated that he would be carried out of reach of the flour bag just at the back of his head, which, suspended at the other end of the crossbar on the post, would swing round when the board was struck. It was also calculated that if the rider did not maintain his pace, he would get a blow from the flour bag just at the back of his head, and bear about him the signs of his awkwardness to the great amusement of the lookers-on.

'Harry Greenacre did not object to being powdered with flour in the service of his mistress. . . But his ability in this respect was not great.' The revival of medieval chivalry was as much a part of the Gothic revival as any new parish church.

Later in Queen Victoria's reign, stoolball, played in the time of Queen Elizabeth, was revived and the rules codified. It was one of the games from which cricket developed, where the 'stool' later became the wicket.

Boys playing with large fancy marbles known as 'taws' in the game of increase pound, one of the illustrations from The Boy's Own Book of Sports and Pastimes, *which was published in 1880. Many of the village children's games were played with marbles in the dirt of the streets and lanes.*

A distended bladder would once have served as a ball in this game, but the Victorian ball was usually made of India rubber. It was so heavy that players wore a leather gauntlet to protect the arm they used to keep the ball in the air, tossing it from one to another.

Winter's ice and snow naturally afforded a great deal of entertainment. Bandy was a kind of ice-hockey, played with curved sticks, or 'bandies', and a small block of wood known as a 'cat'. It was perhaps in the Fens that country people gained the most enjoyment from very cold weather, for there stretches of water would frequently freeze to a depth of several inches for weeks on end. Winters are always said to have been colder in those days. Curling competitions were held, and skaters raced each other along the frozen waterways. In hilly country children amused themselves sledging down the steep snowy slopes.

Curling was a winter sport enjoyed by Victorian men. There were two to a side and each player had two stones with handles which he made skid and curl across the ice towards a 'tee' at the centre of a circle.

The churchyard, a useful open space in the heart of the village, was the scene of ball games of various types. Some of them made use of the exterior features of the church itself – and sometimes, when the players missed, windows got broken. The ball would be thrown or hit against a corner or the space between buttresses and complicated local rules were devised, as they were for games in the school playground.

Children had a whole range of games that were their own, many of them played in some form to this day – tag, leap frog, blind man's buff, pig in the middle, skipping songs, or standing in a ring to play drop the handkerchief:

Another of the outdoor games described in The Boy's Own Book, *which was played with quoits. The rings were hurled at a distant target, and any number could join in.*

> I wrote a letter to my love
> And on the way I dropped it.
> One of you has picked it up
> And put it in his pocket.
> It wasn't you, it wasn't you... it was YOU.

Some of the games belonged to one particular locality, like the Cornish 'snail creep' played at village festivals in June: 'The young people being all assembled in a large meadow, the village band strikes up a simple but lively air and marches forward, followed by the whole assemblage, leading hand-in-hand... The band, or head of the serpent, keeps marching in an ever-narrowing circle... whilst its train of dancing followers becomes coiled round it.' The whole community came out to watch or join in the happy game.

Sliding on the ice was great sport for the children. Sometimes they set obstacles of stones for themselves, which may have caused the tumble pictured below.

FESTIVALS

IN THE EARLY YEARS OF Queen Victoria's reign, it seemed to some, including William Howitt, who complained that 'England is no longer merry England, but busy England', that the occasions for making merry were declining, and only a deliberate revival would sustain them. Perhaps this was truest of all of May Day: setting up the maypole and dancing around it, making garlands of flowers and branches of hawthorn in full bloom, and choosing the Queen of the May became children's rather than young adults' activities. The traditional degree of licence which young men and women enjoyed on that day, and the fertility symbolism of the maypole dances, meant that moralists waged a campaign against the Maying, and had done so ever since the sixteenth century. In the West Riding of Yorkshire, maypole dances and local pride in May Day festivities persisted, however, and vestiges of the merrymaking continued elsewhere. In Huntingdonshire, Howitt reported, there were particularly elaborate celebrations: '. . . the children still exhibit garlands. They suspend a sort of crown of hoops, wreathed and ornamented with flowers, ribbons, handkerchiefs, necklaces, silver spoons, and whatever finery can be procured, at a considerable height above the road, by a rope extending from chimney to chimney of the cottages, while they attempt to throw their balls over it from side to side, singing, and begging halfpence' for a festive tea.

Nevertheless, there seem still to have been plenty of opportunities for making merry in Victorian villages. There were the annual round of church festivals and the regular events in the farming calendar, and from time to time there were occasions of local or national importance to celebrate.

'Fifty years ago 'twere all mirth and jollity,' Arthur Gibb wrote in 1898: 'There was four feasts in the year for us folk. First of all there was the savers' feast – that would be about the end of April; then came the sheep-shearer's feast – there'd be about fifteen of us would sit down after sheep-shearing, and we'd be singing best part of the night, and plenty to eat and drink; next came the feast for the reapers, when the corn was cut about August; and last of all, the harvest home in September.'

May Day: the milk-white of the May Queen and the soot-black of the sweep are contrasting elements in the celebrations in this painting by William Collins. It was traditionally the day of the London sweeps, but they would often appear, clad in grotesque costumes and carrying collecting boxes, in country May Day revelries.

151

The harvest home was originally the principal festivity in the farming year, held after the last load of corn was brought in from the fields. According to its historian, at Wicken in the Cambridgeshire fens, the final load, called the 'horkey', was 'the central feature of a gay procession, its horses decked with bright ribbons and flowers and boughs, while a pair of men *en harlequin* were dressed to represent the sexes'. Afterwards, there was feasting and drinking – 'good fare, nut-brown home-brewed ale, and merry songs' – the farmers sometimes waiting on their employees as a

An Illustrated London News engraving of an elaborate harvest home at Swallowfield in Berkshire. The celebration of harvest safely gathered in was the culmination of the rural calendar. As the last field was cleared, the final wagon was decorated and everyone paraded back to the farmyard chanting, 'Harvest Home! Harvest Home! | We've ploughed, | We've sown, | We've reaped, | We've mown, | Harvest Home! Harvest Home!'

thank offering for their hard work in the fields. In Norfolk, the traditional cry of the harvest revellers for 'Largesse, largesse!' came after the singing of rousing choruses of:

> Here's health to our master, the lord of the feast,
> God bless his endeavours and send him increase
> ... come, drink off your beer.

The largesse was the bonus money given by the farmer to all who had helped with the harvest.

Such scenes did not always accord with Victorian sensibilities, however, and harvest home revelry gradually fell from favour. Instead, the harvest festival was devised, focusing on the church and a more decorous – but none the less heart-felt – celebration. At Wicken, for example, the horkey feast was replaced by afternoon tea, and Rider Haggard in Norfolk in 1899 imagined that the cry of 'Largesse!' would never be heard again. The initiator of the concept of harvest festivals was Robert Stephen Hawker, the eccentric Cornish parson, who instigated the spate of Victorian harvest hymns. Sabine Baring-Gould, Hawker's friend and first biographer, rejoiced: 'The harvest home is no more. We have instead harvest festivals, tea and cake at sixpence a head in the school-room, and a choral service and a sermon in the church... There are no more shearing feasts; what remains are shorn of all their festive character.'

The first festival associated with the farming year came as a day of respite in the winter's depths, and was called Plough Monday. It fell on the first Monday after Twelfth Night, and was the first time after Christmas that ploughing was resumed. It was the ancient custom for farm labourers, tricked out in ribbons and scarves, to drag a plough around the parish calling at doors to ask for money to pay for festivities – drinking, sword-dancing and a mummers' play, which symbolized the end of the old year and the start of the new. Here, too, the Church in Victorian times took part in the festival, usually by having the plough blessed.

Christmas was, of course, the most popular festival of the Church. The Victorians – notably Prince Albert and Charles Dickens – largely invented the type of Christmas celebration we know today, with trees and lights, and the exchange of cards and gifts: all practices that gradually found their way into the countryside. The newer forms of celebration grew up alongside the older ones, which involved the ancient symbols of holly, ivy, mistletoe and the Yule log, and the village waits touring the village in the darkness of evening singing carols and playing their instruments under cottage and farmhouse windows. William Wordsworth evoked the carollers in one of his poems:

> The minstrels played their Christmas tune,
> Tonight beneath my cottage eaves...
> Through hill and valley, every breeze,
> Had sunk to rest with folded wings;
> Keen was the air, but could not freeze,

Well-dressing, an ancient custom in thanksgiving for the purity of water, had survived or been revived in some Victorian villages, perhaps most famously at Tissington in Derbyshire on Ascension Day. The well was elaborately garlanded and decorated with a biblical text for a ceremony led by the clergymen and village choir.

Nor check the music of the strings;
So stout and hardy were the band,
That scraped the chords with strenuous hand!

In many country areas the mummers' plays survived as a Christmas tradition – George and the Dragon was one of the favourites, with figures such as the Turkish knight and much slaying of vanquished foes – just as Thomas Hardy recounted it in *The Return of the Native*:

Make room, make room, my gallant boys,
And give us space to rhyme;
We've come to show Saint George's play,
Upon this Christmas time.

A landlord's Christmas box to his tenants might be a joint of beef, and every household would endeavour to provide something extra: a plum pudding, mincemeat, spiced ales and elderberry wines where they could, or in the poorest families a saved-for orange. Christmas Day was one of the only national holidays until the bank holidays were introduced, largely for town workers, in the 1880s.

The springtime, and mid-Lent, celebration of Mothering Sunday was widely observed. Francis Kilvert recorded on Mothering Sunday 1871 in his Welsh border parish that 'all the country [was] in an upturn going out visiting. Girls and boys going home to see their mothers and taking them cakes, brothers and sisters of middle age going to see each other.' They were regaled with furmity, a favourite rural repast of wheat boiled in milk and seasoned with spices.

Easter and Whitsun were other times for celebration. In many villages, Whitsun was the date set for the Club Day, when the local working men's friendly society would organize a feast – Arthur Gibb's 'savers' feast'. Whitsun was also the traditional time for many parish feasts (which were otherwise held on the feast day of some perhaps long-forgotten local saint). Games would be played and a great meal served, sometimes paid for by the local squire, emblematic of his generosity.

'Mother makes us the Toggery'. The ragged costumes and animal masks being sewn for the children's mumming play in a watercolour by Miss E. D. Herschel of 1887.

Many folk customs were revived by schoolteachers and the clergy. Mumming plays were traditionally performed at Christmas and before the spring sowing. The play to be performed here in Littlemore, Oxfordshire, is St George and the Dragon.

The parish feast saw the whole village *en fête*. A travelling fun fair might arrive and set up for the week, morris dancers perform in their curious costumes, with bells attached to their skirts and cottagers keep open house for the day. In late Victorian Hadden-ham, in Buckinghamshire, 'No institution was more popular, or more deeply rooted in village sentiment, than our annual Feast' in early September, as Walter Rose remembered: 'It was a whole day of festivity, when, from outlying farms, lads and lasses, hired for the year, were given a day's leave and arrived early, buxom and

smiling. Each cottage home was ready for them; the gleaned corn had been ground, the pie of pears had been made from its flour, and a joint of fresh meat had been cooked. . . the thrill of anticipation was in every heart.'

So the round of village festivities continued. In some areas they made a special celebration of Guy Fawkes' Night on 5 November with bonfires, in others of Midsummer Day, or of Michaelmas, the time of the local hiring fairs. Pancake races on Shrove Tuesday, egg rolling on Easter Day, making mischief at Hallowe'en, when witches and evil spirits were held to traverse the earth on their baneful midnight errands, were local customs that were maintained in certain villages. There were also occasional celebrations. Some were personal. Craftsmen might take days off when they felt so inclined, in a tradition known as Saint Monday. Others were public. The national outpourings of jubilation in 1887 and 1897 to celebrate Queen Victoria's fifty and then sixty years on the throne were marked by village festivities

Village Waits, an illustration to a poem by William Wordsworth from a Pictorial Calendar of Seasons, 1854, 'The minstrels played their Christmas tune / Tonight beneath my cottage eaves . . . / Keen was the air, but could not freeze, / Nor check the music of the strings; / So stout and hardy were the band, / That scraped the chords with strenuous hands.'

the length and breadth of the land, with sports and games, parades and the dedication of memorials, inevitably accompanied by a lavishly prepared feast.

A family, and often a whole village, would get caught up in the merrymaking associated with a wedding: a party with music provided by the collected players of the parish and a hearty romp. Some parishes had a separate room or hall where nuptials were celebrated. As they did in Hardy's *Under the Greenwood Tree*, the party-goers, whatever their ages, would forget their cares and enjoy themselves: '. . . a perceptible dampness makes itself apparent upon the faces even of delicate girls – a ghastly dew having for some time rained from the faces of their masculine partners; when skirts begin to be torn out of their gathers; when elderly people, who have stood up to please their juniors, begin to feel sundry small tremblings in the region of the knees.'

It was scenes of revelry like this that enlivened the farming year and punctuated the lives of men, women and children in the Victorian village.

Hunting the wren, a Christmas custom observed in the Isle of Man when the local people would seek out and kill a wren after the midnight prayers on Christmas Eve. The bird was then laid out with much solemnity and brought back to the church to be prayed over and buried.

Letting in Christmas, a tradition from Yorkshire, as depicted in the Illustrated London News *of 1860.*

LETTING IN CHRISTMAS.

VICTORIAN OBSERVERS

MANY NINETEENTH-CENTURY WRITERS devoted themselves to describing the Victorian countryside, in prose and in poetry, through fiction as well as documentary writing. A variety of them have been quoted in the pages of this book. Some, like the novelists George Eliot (1819–80) and Anthony Trollope (1815–82), wrote on a very broad canvas: the countryside tended to form a backdrop to their books. For others, it was the very backbone of their work.

The earliest of them was Mary Russell Mitford. Her father's gambling and extravagance forced her to try to make a living from her pen. In that, she was eminently successful, and her greatest success came from essays that she published, acute, witty and not overly sentimental observations on her home village. Published in book form as *Our Village* in 1832, these are the writings for which Miss Mitford remains famous.

Another observer of the early Victorian countryside was William Howitt. He produced three editions of *The Rural Life of England*, a panoramic survey of country life and ways. Howitt was a sentimental and enthusiastic describer of what he saw in roughly equal proportions, writing about everything he came across on his travels – festivals and fields, gypsies and games, shooting and schooling. He published several books and essays, especially on calendar customs, with engraved vignettes.

The diversity of country life is to be found in the engaging diaries of the Reverend Francis Kilvert. Written in the 1870s, he describes parish life for an impoverished curate and observes life and pretty girls with a keen eye. Kilvert loved his parishioners, and recorded their sayings and their foibles, together with the beauties of the countryside. From 1865 until 1872 he was curate at Clyro, in Radnorshire, and then at Langley Burrell, Wiltshire, for four years. He became vicar at St Harmon in Radnorshire and then at Bredwardine, Herefordshire. This Welsh border area has become immortalized as 'Kilvert Country'.

Dorset has been immortalized as 'Hardy's Wessex'. This was the novelist and poet Thomas Hardy's own deliberate creation. He was born in a woodland cottage at Higher Bockhampton, near

Dorchester, in 1840, the son of a stonemason. In the twenty-four years from 1871 he wrote some of the most powerful of all English fiction, setting his work within a thinly disguised Dorset and surrounding area, for which he revived the name 'Wessex'. The success of *Far from the Madding Crowd* (1874) enabled him to give up architecture to become a full-time writer. Hardy's skill was to weave memories and observations of country life into stories of love and life where the role of Fate was paramount: novels such as *Under the Greenwood Tree* (1872), *Tess of the D'Urbervilles* (1891), and *The Mayor of Casterbridge* (1886).

H. Rider Haggard is famous for such stirring fiction as *King Solomon's Mines* and *She*. In *Rural England* he described the countryside of the 1890s, suffering as it was from long-term depression. In 1899, he published *A Farmer's Year*, his own farming diary and jottings for 1898, about his land on the Norfolk-Suffolk border.

Richard Jefferies left one of the largest bodies of Victorian country writings. His essays, natural history books and novels all showed a poetic imagination and acute observation. In his works, especially *Hodge and his Masters*, published in 1880, and *The Open Air* (1885), he interwove observation of nature and of people into a series of essays that vigorously brought the countryside to life. In *Bevis, the Story of a Boy* (1884), he produced one of the classic children's books, partly reliving his own childhood and its country pursuits in the woods and on the river. Jefferies has become one of the best-loved documentarist writers about the Victorian countryside, and there is today a Richard Jefferies Society.

Two writers who relived their childhood experiences in autobiographical fiction were Flora Thompson and Alison Uttley. Flora Thompson's trilogy *Lark Rise to Candleford* (1939–1943), was the story of her childhood in the Oxfordshire hamlet of Juniper Hill and then work in the post office of the nearby village of Fringford. Although she wrote many other essays and books, it is for this clear-eyed evocation of late Victorian village life that she is remembered. The author of the *Little Grey Rabbit* children's books, Alison Uttley, also wrote a classic memoir of her childhood, *The Country Child* (1931). Brought up on a farm in the Derbyshire hills south of Matlock in the late 1880s and 1890s, she drew upon these memories to write a succession of charming vignettes of her family farm and her local village school and church.

ACKNOWLEDGEMENTS

Bodleian Library, Oxford 46, 154, 155; Bridgeman Art Library 11, 18, 42, 62, 79, 99, 123, 131, 138, 151; Bristol City Art Gallery 78 (Bridgeman Art Library); British Museum 43; Bury Art Gallery 14 (Bridgeman Art Library); Christie's 34, 47, 83, 85; Courtauld Institute of Art 52, 53, 60, 68, 116, 117, 128, 129, 144, 145 (all Witt Library); William Drummond 76; Fine Art Photographs 2, 15, 23, 31, 39, 55, 59, 63, 67, 71, 91, 98, 103, 107, 114, 115, 119, 126, 127, 135, 139; Luton Museum and Art Gallery 51; Mansell Collection 41, 104, 105, 109, 140; Mary Evans Picture Library 152, 156, 157; Marylebone Cricket Club 147 (Bridgeman Art Library); National Gallery of Ireland 122; National Trust 27; Ronan Picture Library 121; Sotheby & Co. 21, 65; Suffolk Record Office 24, 25; Tate Gallery 95; Towner Art Gallery, Eastbourne 35 (Bridgeman Art Library); Townley Art Gallery, Burnley 87 (Bridgeman Art Library); Victoria & Albert Museum 19 (Bridgeman Art Library), 82; Warrington Museum and Art Gallery 106 (Bridgeman Art Library); Wolverhampton Art Gallery 75, 111, 143 (all Bridgeman Art Library); Yale Center for British Art, New Haven 7; York City Art Gallery 54 (Bridgeman Art Library).

Other illustrations come from the following books:

The Book of English Trades (1836) 56, 57, 100, 101; The Boy's Own Book of Sports and Pastimes (1880) 148, 149; J. F. Burke, British Husbandry (1837) 69; P. H. Ditchfield, The Charm of the English Village (1908) 1, 8, 12, 13, 16, 17, 40, 125, 141; W. D. Drury (ed.), The Book of Gardening (1900) 44, 45; Excelsior, Volume III (n.d.) 153; Myles Birket Foster, Pictures of an English Village (1863) 9, 48, 84; M. Howitt, Pictorial Calendar of the Seasons (1849) 108, 156; W. Howitt, The Year-Book of the Country (1850) 61, 120; J. H. Keene, The Practical Fisherman (1881) 108, 109; J. Larwood and J. C. Hotten, The History of Signboards (1867) 124; J. C. Loudon, Encyclopedia of Agriculture (1844) 73, 79; J. C. Loudon, Encyclopedia of Cottage, Farm and Villa Architecture (1857) 28, 29, 36, 37; T.Nutt, Humanity to Honey Bees (1832) 49; W. H. Pyne, Costume of Great Britain (1808) 128, 144, 145; W. H. Pyne, Microcosm (1806) 76, 77, 96, 97, 112, 113, 120, 132, 133, 134, 135, 136, 137; P. F. Robinson, Village Architecture (1830) 16, 17, 64; Stephens' Book of the Farm (5th edition, 1908) 72, 88, 89; Lord Walsingham and Sir R. Payne-Gallwey, Shooting (1888) 32, 33; W. Youatt, The Complete Grazier (1877) 80, 81, 92, 93.